QM Medical Libraries

24 1007163 C

D0129973

BARTS AND THE LONDON

SCHOOL OF MEDICINE AND DENTISTRY

WHITECHAPEL LIBRARY,TURNER STREET, LONDON E1 2AD
020 7882 7110

ONE WEEK LOAN

Book are to be returned on or before the last date below,
otherwise fines may be charged.

2 7 APR 2005

2 5 MAR 2009

2 9 SEP 2005

3 1 MAR 200

2 2 MAY 2006

2 1 APR 2008

WITHDRAWN
FROM STOCK
QMUL LIBRARY

By the same author

The Art of Psychotherapy

Second Edition

ANTHONY STORR FRCP FRCPsych

WITHDRAWN
FROM STOCK
QMUL LIBRARY

ARNOLD

A member of the Hodder Headline Group
LONDON • NEW YORK • NEW DELHI

This edition first published in Great Britain in 1990 by Butterworth Heinemann.

This impression published in 2002 and reprinted in 2004 by
Arnold, a member of the Hodder Headline Group,
338 Euston Road, London NW1 3BH

http://www.arnoldpublishers.com

Distributed in the USA by
Oxford University Press Inc.,
198 Madison Avenue, New York, NY 10016
Oxford is a registered trademark of Oxford University Press

CLASS N. WM420 STO

CIRC TYPE 1 WK

SUPPLIER cisc. 19 1 104

READING L K19.99

© Anthony Storr 1979, 1990

All rights reserved. No part of this publication may be reproduced or
transmitted in any form or by any means, electronically or mechanically,
including photocopying, recording or any information storage or retrieval
system, without either prior permission in writing from the publisher or a
licence permitting restricted copying. In the United Kingdom such licences
are issued by the Copyright Licensing Agency: 90 Tottenham Court Road,
London W1P 0LP.

Whilst the advice and information in this book are believed to be true and
accurate at the date of going to press, neither the authors nor the publisher
can accept any legal responsibility or liability for any errors or omissions
that may be made. In particular (but without limiting the generality of the
preceding disclaimer) every effort has been made to check drug dosages;
however, it is still possible that errors have been missed. Furthermore,
dosage schedules are constantly being revised and new side-effects
recognized. For these reasons the reader is strongly urged to consult the
drug companies' printed instructions before administering any of the drugs
recommended in this book.

British Library Cataloguing in Publication Data
A catalogue record for this book is available from the British Library

Library of Congress Cataloging-in-Publication Data
A catalog record for this book is available from the Library of Congress

ISBN 0 7506 0428 X

2 3 4 5 6 7 8 9 10

Printed and bound in Malta by Gutenberg Press

What do you think about this book? Or any other Arnold title?
Please send your comments to feedback.arnold@hodder.co.uk

Contents

Preface to the Second Edition

On re-reading this book ten years after its first appearance, I was surprised that I did not want to alter more of it. Dr Michael Hobbs, who succeeded me in Oxford when I retired, made a number of useful suggestions for which I am grateful. The major changes are that Chapter 11, *The Obsessional Personality*, has been rewritten; and a final Chapter 15, *Solitude, Interests and Healing* has been added. I have also taken to heart certain criticisms which were made of my references to hypnotism in Chapter 3, and amended this passage accordingly.

I have felt for a long time that persons suffering from the severer forms of obsessional neurosis, which can be totally crippling, are in a different diagnostic category from neurotics of obsessional personality who suffer from the milder forms of depression, tension and anxiety. Research seems to support this; and so Chapter 11 has been modified.

The new Chapter 15 reflects my recent interest in those mental processes which take place in solitude.[1] Individual psychotherapy is an interaction between two people, the patient and the therapist. Because the process of psychotherapy is so compelling, both psychotherapists and patients tend to overemphasise the importance of the therapeutic hours, and to forget that significant mental events and changes take place outside the therapist's office. Patients can learn to explore their own psychological processes when they are alone, often with considerable benefit. In doing so, they are following illustrious examples. Both Freud and Jung owed more to their own self-analyses than they did to any colleague with whom they may have discussed their problems.

Ten years ago, one colleague who reviewed *The Art of Psychotherapy* questioned my belief, expressed in the Introduction, that we shall soon see the disappearance of the analytical schools as discrete entities. He felt, as I do not, that belief in some system, be it Freudian, Jungian, Kleinian, or other, was an essential part of the analyst's emotional and intellectual equipment. Although fundamentalist analysts who believe that one or other school has 'the truth' about human nature, and that all others fall short of this, still exist, my observation suggests that this phenomenon is gradually disappearing. For example, my short book 'Freud' in the 'Past Masters' series,[2] is sharply critical as well as appreciative of the founding father of modern psychotherapy. I expected that dedicated Freudians would accuse me of lèse-majesté and lack of insight; but modern Freudians are more ready to accept that Freud had flaws than were their forebears of thirty years ago, and have treated me with generosity. Psychotherapists do not need to subscribe to a doctrinal system, although they do need to have trust in the healing powers both of the therapeutic relationship and of the mind itself.

What is the future of psychotherapy? Predictions are always dangerous and often wrong; but here are my guesses. In spite of all the doubts about the efficacy of psychotherapy which have been expressed since Eysenck first attacked psychoanalysis in the 1950s, I am sure that some varieties of psychotherapy are here to stay. It can be argued that many of the problems in living for which people today seek psychotherapeutic help ought to be relievable by family or friends. I do not agree. People who are neurotically distressed need not only support and sympathy, but also the objective comprehension which only a trained therapist can provide. If a person is to alter, and to learn how better to deal with his problems, he must be given an objective basis of knowledge about himself which goes beyond the acceptance which any sympathiser can provide. Psychotherapists require professional training, and serious emotional problems require professional treatment.

When I was young, psychotherapy was often recommended for disorders for which it no longer seems appropriate. In Chapter 13, I suggest that psychotherapists are best at treating 'the inhibited, the shy, the self-distrustful, the fragmented, the over-dependent, and the over-controlled.' Further research will define these categories more exactly; and I think we shall see the development of new techniques for treating those patients with behaviour disorders with whom psychotherapists have been less successful. These are the patients to whom I refer as 'those who lack control over their impulses, and who "act out" their emotional conflicts.' In the last chapter, I mention recent work which indicates that such disturbances may be better treated by techniques based on reducing environmental stimulation.

Psychoanalysis bade goodbye to science in 1896. In this year, Freud published a paper on hysteria based on eighteen cases; the last attempt he made to give figures concerning aetiology. However, the gulf between science and psychotherapy is gradually being bridged; not only by those who pursue research into outcome, but also by John Bowlby and his followers, who combine psychoanalytic insight with objective studies of attachment and child behaviour. This kind of approach holds out the best promise for the future. We need to understand the complexities of early human growth and development far more completely than we do; and Bowlby's use of concepts derived from ethology has already provided new insights and new techniques of research. Psychoanalysis has always assumed that the environment of the child's first few years was vitally important for its future adjustment. But we need to know, as objectively as possible, how far the disadvantages left by unfortunate or unhappy childhoods can be surmounted as life goes on.

The general public does not realise the extent of our ignorance. At the time of writing, for example, we still have to confess that we do not know the frequency of child sexual abuse, nor the extent to which such abuse damages the child's prospects for making rewarding adult relationships. Some children never recover: others ride the storm successfully. What is amply clear is that the frequency of such abuse has been considerably underestimated.

I also think that further studies along the lines of George Brown's work on *Social Origins of Depression*,[3] will influence the development of psychotherapy. Psychoanalysis has been primarily concerned with exploring the patient's inner world of phantasy, and has tended to neglect the importance of social factors as causes of symptoms. Poverty, bad housing, and actual losses and traumata are more important precipitants of neurotic symptoms than psychoanalysis had realised. Only when such factors have been taken into account and, where possible corrected, can we isolate the problems which are best dealt with by psychotherapy.

As I indicate in the final chapter, I also think that the psychotherapy of the future will be more concerned than it is at present with tapping the patient's own creative potential. Study of the creatively gifted often demonstrates that, however disturbed in mind they may have been, their creative capacities served to protect them against breakdown. We cannot all be writers or painters or composers, but every human being has some creative capacity, some ability to transcend conflict in symbolic fashion. Modern man tends to escape his problems by turning to drugs or drink, or by distracting himself with passive entertainment. The ease with which we can turn on the television set may, in some instances, prevent the realisation of creative capacities for solving conflict, just as it hampers children's capacity for creative play.

The essence of the psychoanalytic method developed by Freud was based on helping the patient to help himself rather than giving him advice, telling him what to do, or issuing prescriptions for living. Psychotherapy can go further in this direction. Jung's technique, originally developed for what he called his 'advanced' patients, of encouraging them to set aside time in which they allowed their phantasies free rein and thus entered into a dialogue with the neglected irrational, emotional springs of their being, can be applied to a wider range of people than Jung envisaged. I anticipate that the psychotherapy of the future will emphasise the importance of the individual's own inner resources, as well as striving to improve his capacity to make intimate relationships.

The readership for whom the book is designed remains the same: postgraduate doctors who are training to become psychiatrists, and other members of the 'helping' professions who need an introduction to the practice of psychotherapy. New techniques and new approaches to psychotherapy are certainly on the way; but, if this book continues to be found useful for a few more years, I shall be well contented.

References
1.   Storr, Anthony (1988) *Solitude*. New York: Free Press. London: Collins (1989).
2.   Storr, Anthony (1989) *Freud*. Oxford: Oxford University Press.
3.   Brown, George W. and Harris, Tirril (1978) *Social Origins of Depression*. London: Tavistock.

Acknowledgements

Professor Michael Gelder, Professor Neil Kessel and Dr Sidney Bloch read the manuscript. Each made valuable suggestions for which I am grateful. I also wish to thank Miss Monica Waud, who typed the greater part of the manuscript; and her colleagues, Miss Marianne Petts, Mrs Jenny Burton and Mrs Beverley Haggis who typed the remainder.

Introduction

This book is intended to provide an introduction to the practice of psychotherapy. It is aimed primarily at postgraduate doctors who are embarking upon specialist training with a view to becoming psychiatrists. It is not intended to be a guide toward passing examinations, although those who read it may find parts of it useful in answering questions about psychotherapy in such examinations as the M.R.C.Psych. What it is intended to be is a practical manual. Faced with a patient who has been referred for psychotherapy, the inexperienced doctor may often feel nonplussed. 'What on earth am I supposed to *do*?', he may ask. This book is intended to provide him with an answer to this question.

Psychotherapy, as I define it, is the art of alleviating personal difficulties through the agency of words and a personal, professional relationship. The kind of psychotherapy about which I am writing, therefore, is analytical and individual, and involves only two participants, the patient and the psychotherapist. Those who want information about group psychotherapy, family therapy, marital therapy, psychodrama, Gestalt therapy or about any of the other myriad forms of psychological intervention will have to look elsewhere.

Individual, analytical psychotherapy is based upon procedures which originated with Freud, who may be called the father of modern psychotherapy. Since Freud began his work, psychotherapy has developed in different directions, with the consequence that there are still a number of 'schools' to which specialist psychotherapists profess allegiance. I myself was originally trained in the school of Jung, to whose ideas I still owe a considerable debt, as may be seen in what follows in this book and also in my short book 'Jung' in the 'Modern Masters' series.[1] However, I have also learned much from a period of analysis with a Freudian, and I have been influenced by the writings of W. R. D. Fairbairn, D. W. Winnicott, Marion Milner, Charles Rycroft, R. D. Laing and Thomas Szasz, to name only a few of the analytical authors. I also owe a great deal to my general psychiatric training, and to my reading in other spheres.

It is my belief that we shall soon see the disappearance of the analytical schools as discrete entities. Although personal analysis will continue to be an important part of training for those who wish to specialise in psychotherapy, the labels of 'Jungian', 'Kleinian', 'Freudian', will become less and less important as research discloses the common factors which lead to a successful outcome in psychotherapy, which, to my mind, is largely independent of the school to which the psychotherapist belongs.

Psychotherapy, both for the patient and for the therapist, is an individual, personal matter; and any book which seeks to convey something of what actually goes on during psychotherapy, rather than listing and discussing the varieties of approach, is bound to be idiosyncratic, and perhaps to appear arrogantly didactic. I am well aware that my particular way of conducting psychotherapy is not the only one. No psychotherapist, and no system or theory has 'the key' to understanding human beings. But I think that it is possible to assert some general principles about the practice of psychotherapy with which the majority of psychotherapists would agree, however they might argue about points of theory; and this is what I have tried to do in this book.

The definition of psychotherapy which I have given above may surprise those who think of psychotherapy primarily as a means of curing neurotic symptoms. When Freud began treating neurotic patients in Vienna toward the end of the nineteenth century, abolition of neurotic symptoms was certainly his primary aim, and his patients, though not suffering from physical disease, resembled medical patients closely enough to be labelled 'ill'. Today, psychotherapists are consulted by people whose symptoms are ill-defined and who are not 'sick' or 'ill' in any conventional, medical sense. They present what Szasz has quite properly called 'problems in living'; and what they are seeking is self-knowledge, self-acceptance, and better ways of managing their lives. Psychotherapy, today, is therefore more concerned with understanding persons as wholes and with changing attitudes than with abolishing symptoms direct. This change in emphasis is further discussed in a later chapter on 'Cure, Termination, and Results'.

Until recently, psychotherapy was largely in the hands of private practitioners; and only those with money could afford any prolonged exploration of their personal problems. Psychiatrists employed by the National Health Service were primarily concerned with the care and treatment of the psychotic, and therefore tended to be more *au fait* with physical methods of treatment than with psychotherapy. However, since psychiatry has increasingly moved from the confines of the mental hospital to the outpatient clinic and the general hospital, psychiatrists within the Health Service have had to become more and more concerned with the treatment of neurosis, and the Royal College of Psychiatrists has recognised that psychiatrists in training require experience and instruction in psychotherapy even if they do not intend to become specialists in this field of psychiatry.

Many of those who become psychiatrists are temperamentally unsuited to the practice of psychotherapy as a whole-time occupation. Indeed, for reasons which I shall discuss later, I am not sure that anyone should practise psychotherapy all day and every day without recourse to teaching, research, writing, or some other alternative way of spending some of his working hours. But even those psychiatrists who are not primarily drawn toward the practice of psychotherapy ought to have some experience of it; and may find, to their surprise, that they are more successful psychotherapists than they had imagined that they could be.

In this book I shall not be writing about the kind of analysis which requires five sessions per week. Even orthodox Freudians seldom see their patients so frequently; and, under the conditions of hospital practice within the National Health Service, such concentrated therapy is virtually impossible. But much valuable therapy can be done on a once or twice weekly basis; and it is this kind of psychotherapy which I shall be discussing for the most part. Although there are some patients who may, for a time, need more frequent sessions, many neurotics can gain considerable benefit from being seen only once or twice weekly; especially if, as I shall later point out, they are encouraged to explore their own psychopathology in the intervals between sessions by writing, painting, talking into a tape-recorder or by any other means that seem appropriate. In fact, there is no evidence that I know of to suggest that the results obtained by five times weekly analysis are superior to those achieved by less intensive therapy; and something to be said against very frequent sessions on the grounds that it encourages a too great dependence upon the therapist and the therapeutic situation.

I turn now to a consideration of the setting in which psychotherapy is, or should be, conducted.

Reference
1.   Storr, Anthony (1973) *Jung*. London: Fontana, Modern Masters.

1

The Setting

In the practice of psychotherapy a number of what appear to be inessential details are in fact important. Thus, the room in which the therapist sees patients, and the way that room is arranged are factors which ought to be taken into consideration. In private practice, one is free to arrange and furnish one's consulting room in any way one likes. In hospital practice, junior doctors are lucky if they have any choice in either the location of the room in which they see patients or in its furnishing or appearance. In spite of this, I shall describe how I think a room in which one is to practise psychotherapy should be; and I would urge all psychotherapists in hospitals and outpatient clinics to insist that these basic requirements are met by the authorities, and to express dissatisfaction when they are not. At present, it is often easier to get money for expensive electrical devices, video-tape recorders, computers and the like than to see that a number of rooms in a psychiatric hospital are properly furnished and sufficiently comfortable for psychotherapy to be carried out.

Ideally, a room in which psychotherapy is to be undertaken should be furnished as follows. First, there should be a comfortable chair in which the patients can relax. Many patients will be so tense at first that they will be unable to make proper use of such a chair; but one hopes that as the therapy progresses they will increasingly be able to do so. Being perched on the edge of a hard chair of the kind too often provided for outpatients is not conducive to personal revelation, and may put the patient at a disadvantage compared with the doctor, who will almost certainly be more comfortably seated.

Second, there should be a couch on which the patient can lie down. This should *not* be an examination couch of the kind which physicians use for physical examinations, but something far more comfortable. When I was in private practice I used a divan bed which proved satisfactory. If suitably covered, this does not look like a bed, to which some patients might object, and which others might welcome with misplaced enthusiasm. It should have at its foot end an extra piece of the same material in which it is covered, which can easily be removed for cleaning. This enables the patient to lie down without having to take off his shoes, which might otherwise dirty the cover.

At the other end of the couch should be a number of suitably covered cushions which the patient can arrange in any way that he finds comfortable.

The couch should be so placed that the therapist can sit at the head end of it, out of sight of the patient, without having to rearrange the furniture every time the couch is used.

Many psychotherapists never follow the psychoanalytical practice of using a couch, for reasons which I shall later discuss. But I have found it useful with some patients; and I prefer to have it as an available alternative which the patient can use if he finds it easier to relax when lying down, or easier to talk if he is not face-to-face with the therapist.

In most clinic rooms, the doctor will be provided with a desk, and with a more or less comfortable chair in which he will sit behind it. This arrangement has the disadvantage that it immediately puts the doctor in a 'superior' position vis-à-vis the patient; but does enable the doctor easily to take notes if he wishes to do so. When one has had the opportunity of getting to know a patient really well over a period of time, taking notes may be superfluous: but most doctors will want to do so initially, though they should not do so if the patient objects. Note-taking should be as unobtrusive as possible, in order not to interrupt the patient's discourse.

It is important that, if the doctor is sitting behind a desk, the furniture be so arranged that the patient is not immediately opposite him, with the desk intervening like an impassable barrier. Business tycoons use their desks as means of intimidating their juniors, which is why they often insist upon having unnecessarily large expanses of mahogany between them and their 'inferiors'. It is generally possible so to arrange the furniture that, if a desk is used, the patient's chair is placed to one side of it, so that there is little feeling of a barrier. Which side is chosen depends upon whether the therapist writes with his left hand or his right. I happen to write with my right hand, and therefore place the patient on my left. This enables me to scribble notes if I wish to do so, whilst at the same time facing the patient and being able to say things directly to him without turning away or looking down. A therapist who writes with his left hand would find the opposite arrangement appropriate.

It is useful to have one or two extra chairs easily available in case it may be necesssary to see relatives together with the patient. In individual psychotherapy, which is the kind of psychotherapy with which I am primarily concerned, such interviews will normally be confined to the initial meeting with the patient; but there are exceptions, and it is therefore wise to be prepared to seat one or two more people when needed.

In hospital, it is probable that the therapist, especially when he is beginning, will have little choice in how the room is decorated or in what other furniture may be there. Hospital rooms are often drab, suggesting impersonal officialdom and the 'Welfare' State. I do not believe that it is necessarily more expensive to decorate a room in such a way that it gives the impression of warmth and friendliness. Where the therapist is in a position to exercise his own personal choice, he may well like to hang some pictures on the walls, and fill the bookshelves (if there are any) with his own books. This is entirely reasonable; but I think it important, for reasons which will emerge later, that the room should not contain anything which too stridently asserts the therapist's taste or which is likely to reveal a great deal of his personal life. Suppose, for example, that the therapist is a devout Catholic. If his bookshelf is full of devotional works and there is a crucifix upon the wall, he is likely to alienate the patient who is agnostic or a convinced Protestant; and he may find that some patients become guarded in their speech for fear of offending the therapist's religious sensibilities.

Many professional people like to bring reminders of home into their offices by displaying photographs of their wives and children. I think it is undesirable for psychotherapists to do this. When patients become deeply involved in the psychotherapeutic process, they are likely to experience powerful feelings of love, hate, envy, jealousy and the like toward the therapist. Explicit reminders of the therapist's life outside the consulting room of the kind provided by family photographs may inhibit the expression of these feelings. Moreover, the patient will certainly have phantasies about the therapist's personal life; and the content of these phantasies may be important in understanding the patient. For example, a patient may express the phantasy that the therapist is homosexual, and exploration of this phantasy is likely to reveal something about the patient's own homosexual interests. A photograph of the therapist's wife and children is likely to act as a constant reminder of his heterosexuality, and thus may inhibit the patient's phantasy, or arouse envy. Female patients may compare themselves, favourably or unfavourably, with the woman depicted in the photograph; and, whilst this may prove to be a valuable piece of exploration of the patient's psyche, it is likely to cause more resentment on the part of the therapist than would be the case if the patient's idea of his wife and children was based only upon supposition.

It is important that, if possible, the room should be quiet. Extraneous noise is not only disturbing in itself, but also gives rise to anxiety on the part of the patient. For if noise from without can come into the room, it is likely that sounds from within can be heard outside it. Nothing is more inimical to frank disclosure than the belief that one may be overheard. Most hospital rooms will contain a telephone. It is most important that, during the time of a psychotherapeutic session, the therapist does not make or take telephone calls. This is usually possible to arrange, except when the doctor is on call for emergency duties within the hospital. In my view, the doctor practising psychotherapy should do so only on those days on which he is not on call for emergencies, or else ensure that a colleague covers for him during the time during which he is practising psychotherapy. If he is furnished with a 'bleep' he should discard it during therapeutic sessions, and explain to those on duty at the telephone switchboard that he will not be available during this particular period.

It is often hard to convince telephone operators and secretaries that one really must not be disturbed during psychotherapy sessions.'But Dr X said it was urgent,' they will protest. Calls are very seldom so urgent that they cannot be postponed for fifty minutes (to put it at its worst), or transferred to someone else. When I was in practice in London, I was so insistent upon not being disturbed that when a call came through from a doctor in Australia, my receptionist told him to ring back later. I congratulated her upon her firmness. It is important so to arrange the times of psychotherapeutic sessions that there is a gap of ten minutes or longer between patients. This enables the therapist to deal with telephone calls or other matters which may have arisen during the session with the last patient.

All these things are much more easily arranged in private practice than in hospital practice. My view is that, whether the patient is paying for treatment directly by paying private fees, or indirectly by the taxation which finances the Health Service, he is entitled to feel that the time he spends with the therapist is *his* time; and that this should not be diminished by interruptions.

2

The Initial Interview

How does one begin psychotherapy? Before the therapist has become experienced, he may well feel somewhat apprehensive at having a new patient referred to him for treatment. Will he be able to do anything to help? Will he be able to understand what the patient is talking about? Will the patient realise his inexperience? What will the patient think of him? These apprehensions, and others which are similar, are to a certain extent justified. The therapist is likely to be confronted with a wide variety of people with whose style of life and mode of expression he is not necessarily familiar, from kitchen porters to university teachers. Many of the patients he sees will be older than he is, and some will be more intelligent. All this matters less than the inexperienced therapist commonly supposes. Provided that he is genuinely interested in the patient as a person, he is likely to be able to overcome any initial difficulties which unfamiliarity with the patient's type of social background may pose. Occasionally, if the patient comes from an entirely different culture, the basic social assumptions of the therapist and patient may be so widely discrepant that communication becomes impossible, but this is rare. Such problems will be discussed at a later point. Let us for the moment assume that the therapist has referred to him a patient who does not present any obvious problem in communication. How shall he go about conducting the first interview with such a patient?

In the U.S.A. and some other countries, people seeking help

with their personal problems will often present themselves directly to a psychotherapist. In Great Britain, more particularly within the National Health Service, it is likely that the patient will have consulted his family doctor and been referred to a consultant psychiatrist for assessment. If the latter adjudges him suitable, he will pass him on to the psychotherapist. This means that the therapist will have in front of him a letter about the patient, and such notes as the consultant may have made. He will also have the letter of referral from the patient's general practitioner. In addition, there may be notes from an interview with a social worker, and reports of tests carried out by a clinical psychologist.

The therapist ought to familiarise himself with this material *before* the time of the first appointment with the patient. If he does not do this, he will either find himself reading the notes during the first interview instead of using this vital period for getting to know the patient, or he will keep the patient waiting unnecessarily. Both practices are undesirable. In ordinary social life, one would not dream of diverting one's attention from a new acquaintance to read a book or a newspaper; and, when a guest arrives, it is usual to greet him at once. Why should one treat a patient differently? Indeed, one ought to be *more* scrupulous about treating patients with courtesy than one is in social life with one's friends. Many patients are alarmed by doctors, especially by psychiatrists. Confiding in strangers is not easy; and the patient who has been sitting apprehensively in a waiting-room for longer than he needs is less likely to be at ease when the new doctor finally sees him.

It is important to remember that, since most patients referred for psychotherapy will have seen at least two doctors before, and may also have seen a social worker and a psychologist, they may well be resentful at being passed on to yet another practitioner. I find this reaction entirely understandable. In our age of specialisation, it is unavoidable; but many patients are unfamiliar with the way the system works, and feel that they are being pushed from pillar to post in an arbitrary fashion.

When the patient is shown in, or is fetched by the therapist from a waiting room, it is courteous to greet him by his name. 'Mr Robinson? Good morning. I'm Dr X'. This both establishes that the therapist actually knows the patient's name, and also indicates that he is to be treated as a person, not merely as a numbered case. In many instances, especially if the patient seems ill-at-ease or suspicious, it it helpful to add: 'Dr Z (the name of the consultant whom the patient has already seen) has asked me to see you regularly for a while, in order to see if we can sort out some of your problems together'.

The point of this remark is, first, to establish that the therapist appreciates that the patient may not understand why he has been passed on to yet another doctor; and, second, to convey to the patient, right from the start, that psychotherapy is a joint enterprise rather than a series of interviews in which the patient is given instructions or advice, as happens in ordinary medical consultations.

Having invited the patient to sit down in a chair appropriately placed in the way already described, what does the therapist do next? He is already faced with a dilemma. Should he, or should he not, take a history? The patient will already have given his history at length to at least two other doctors, and maybe to many more if he has been referred from another department in the hospital. He is likely to assume that the nature of his complaint and the details of his personal and family history are known to this new doctor by whom he is confronted; and is justified in this assumption in that, as I have said, the therapist should have read the notes before he sees the patient. Many patients resent giving their history yet again, and often say so. However, as every doctor knows or should know, other doctors' notes are much less helpful than one's own. Moreover, they are much less easily remembered. Taking one's own history from a patient gives one an unrivalled opportunity of assessing what a particular symptom *means* to the patient; something which is difficult to convey in notes or letters. When a person talks to one about his family and his past experience, his tone of voice, the phraseology he uses, whether he looks at one or hangs his head, may be revealing in a way which medical notes are not. Only the greatest novelists can make people come alive for us in writing; and it is too much to hope that consultant psychiatrists can achieve this.

It used to be the fashion for psychoanalysts not to take histories. Instead, their practice was, even at a first interview, to instruct the patient to lie upon the couch and then to proceed to say whatever occurred to him. This practice may be possible in the case of patients who are familiar with psychoanalytic procedure, and who therefore know what is expected of them, but is not suitable for those who are less sophisticated. Moreover, the psychoanalyst who adopts this procedure runs the risk of missing important information. I once treated a patient who suffered from depression who had seen so many doctors before she came to me that I did not take a formal history. I cannot remember – I am ashamed to remember – how long I had been seeing her before I realised that, instead of being the virginal person I had supposed, she had had a very large number of affairs with men about which she was extremely reticent.

I am therefore in favour of the therapist taking his own history, however many times the patient may have given it to other people. I usually say to the patient; 'I've read your notes and I have some idea of your background and your present trouble, but I would be grateful if you would go over some of it again. I know that you have told it all before to various people, and that it must be very tedious for you to repeat it, but I find it difficult to remember details from notes made by other people. I understand that your present trouble is depression (or whatever the patient's main complaint may be). Could we start there? What is your kind of depression really like?'

This kind of approach usually dispels any feeling of resentment which the patient may have at being asked to repeat himself.

However, the therapist should feel free to take a rather different kind of history from that which the consultant has already provided, and from that which he himself is used to taking at diagnostic interviews or in other branches of medicine. In diagnostic interviews, when time is limited, and decisions have immediately to be made, doctors are trained to obtain essentials, to ask a great many questions, and to follow formal schemes of enquiry which ensure that they do not omit anything which may be vital. Present complaint; previous illnesses; family history; personal history; use of drugs, tobacco, and alcohol, and so on. Such schemes of enquiry may be so elaborate (as in the case of that devised at the Maudsley Hospital) that to obtain answers to all the questions listed would take many hours. Medical students and inexperienced doctors often become anxious because they have not been able to note answers to all the questions they have been trained to ask. Consequently, they interrupt the flow of the patient's discourse, and constantly attempt to pin him down when what *he* wants to talk about may be something entirely different.

Although the psychotherapist should take a history from the patient at his initial interview with him, he has the advantage of already being familiar with the formal details of the patient's past and present. Thus, he will already know whether or not the patient is married; whether his parents are alive or dead; how many siblings he has; and whether he has any children. He will also have an outline of his childhood development and previous illnesses. He is therefore free to let the patient wander; to encourage him to expand upon topics which he did not have time to deal with in previous interviews. Suppose, for example, that the patient described his father as 'strict', and that this bare description has been dutifully recorded in the notes. The psychotherapist, when he reaches the point in his history taking at which the patient's relationship with his parents is being discussed, may enquire: 'I see you describe your father as having been strict. Can you tell me more about this? In what way was he strict? Give me some examples.'

When a novelist wants to make his characters come alive, he will usually depict them in action. Just telling the reader that so and so was mean or courageous or cruel will not bring the character to life so vividly as will incident. We remember Mr Murdstone's vicious flogging of David Copperfield with greater clarity than we remember his appearance or speech. In the same way, we remember incidents from the patient's past which illustrate his behaviour and relations with others more vividly than we recall mere adjectival descriptions. Suppose, for example, that the patient with a strict father tells us that the latter was very particular about what time he came in at night. 'Once, I came in five minutes after the time I was supposed to be in by. There was my father, watch in hand, waiting up for me. I shall never forget how frightened I was. I expected him to hit me; but what he did was to dock my pocket money; so much for every minute I was late.' Such an anecdote is far more revealing of the character of the patient's father, and of the patient's relation with him, than is the label 'strict'. Yet, in a diagnostic interview, it is extremely unlikely that a busy consultant will have been able to give the patient time to recall such incidents.

The psychotherapist's initial interview with a new patient should last for the same length of time as he plans that subsequent interviews should last. Some therapists prefer that the initial interviews should be longer – perhaps twice as long – as subsequent interviews. Such a procedure gives the therapist a better opportunity of getting to know his new patient quickly, but carries the disadvantage of giving the patient false expectations. He may think that all subsequent interviews are to be as long as the first; or, if he feels he needs more time at any particular interview, that the therapist will easily be able to give it to him. As both expectations are false, it is advisable not to arouse them. The initial interview, like those which follow, should last between fifty minutes and an hour. This period of time may seem arbitrary, but this is not so. Shorter interviews are apt to be frustrating, both for the therapist and patient, in that not enough time is allowed for topics to be pursued in depth. Longer interviews, though both patient and therapist may sometimes want them, are apt to be tiring for both parties. Psychotherapy, properly carried out, requires concentration and alertness; and most of us know, from experience of lectures, that attention is difficult to sustain without a break beyond a time-span of forty-five to fifty minutes. The fifty-minute hour, now hallowed by tradition, allows the therapist to make appointments on the hour, and gives him ten minutes between each patient to collect his thoughts, deal with telephone messages, or have a cup of coffee; all of which may be essential in a day in which he is seeing a series of patients.

The psychotherapist should try to bring his initial interview with a patient to an end by the time forty minutes have passed. This is in order to allow time for subsequent appointments to be arranged. It would be convenient both for the psychotherapist and for his patient if, at this point, the number of sessions could be decided. 'How long shall I need to go on coming?' is a reasonable question for the patient to ask, but it is not one which can be answered immediately. What I usually do is to say that, at this early stage, I cannot tell, but that I suggest that we meet on six occasions and then review the situation. Although, by the sixth session, it may still not be possible to give an accurate prediction of the number of sessions needed, this probationary period is usually long enough for the therapist and the patient to decide whether or not they are likely to be able to work fruitfully together.

It is also helpful, at this initial interview, to tell the patient what the length of each session will be. I have suggested fifty minutes, for the reasons given above.

How frequent the sessions should be is a question which, unfortunately, must often be decided by expediency. Ideally, I think that a new patient should be seen three times per week; but, since psychotherapy is a scarce resource, this is seldom possible within the National Health Service in Great Britain. However, good results can often be achieved if the patient is seen only once or twice per week. If sessions are less frequent than this it becomes much more difficult to get to know the patient intimately, to remember what he says from one session to the next, or to maintain a sense of continuity in the therapeutic process.

Ideally, the patient should be asked to come to the same room at the same time of day for each appointment. This not only makes it easier for him to recall the time and place, but also induces a sense of security. If a patient is seen in a series of different rooms, time will be wasted while he looks around and accustoms himself to the strange environment. Once a patient has become used to a particular room, he is more easily able to pay full attention to what is going on within his mind. If a patient is being seen more often than once a week, it will often not be possible to arrange that he be seen at the same time of day on each appointment. It is helpful to have a card on which appointment times are listed in order that no disputes arise about what has been arranged. If a patient misses an appointment, it may be because of his reluctance to face some of his problems, or for other psychological reasons. It may also be because he was not clear about the arrangements made. Putting those arrangements in writing obviates argument. When patients want to alter appointments for what seem to be good reasons, the psychotherapist should seek to accommodate them, if he can do so without too much inconvenience. On the other hand, the wish to alter appointments can be a testing-out by the patient of how compliant the therapist will be. In most instances, it is easy enough to see when an ulterior motive of this kind is operating. The therapist need not punish himself by being too accommodating. On the other hand, he need not punish the patient by being inflexible.

When arrangements for future appointments have been made, some patients, particularly those who are uninformed about psychiatry, may ask what the point of such future meetings may be. Expecting medicines or electricity or some other dramatic intervention, they may say: 'But what is going to happen, doctor? Is it just going to be talk?' In answer to this very natural question I usually reply: 'You have had these problems for some time. If we are going to understand them together, it is necessary for us to go into them in a lot of detail. This is why we must meet on a number of occasions.' This kind of statement is usually adequate to reassure the puzzled patient for the moment. If subsequent meetings go well, he will probably never ask such a question again, as 'just talk' will have acquired a new meaning for him.

The other question which often arises in a first interview is that of confidentiality. Patients in psychotherapy are asked to reveal intimate personal details about themselves which they may never have confided to any other person. It is natural that they should be anxious about who may have access to this intimate material. For the inexperienced therapist two separate questions arise. First, it is possible, indeed desirable, that his treatment of patients is being supervised. Should he reveal to the patient that what he says is being discussed with another doctor (or, if the therapist is part of a group, with other doctors)? I think he should. We require that patients should be honest with us. Should we not lay upon ourselves an equal obligation?

Most patients will accept the notion that their case is being discussed from time to time with a more experienced, senior doctor or with other colleagues. What is the therapist to say if they object? I have not encountered this problem in reality, but I suggest that if it does occur, the therapist suggests that the patient has an interview with the senior doctor or leader of the group with whom his problems are to be discussed. This should serve to allay the patient's anxiety.

Much more troublesome is the question of case-notes. In hospitals many different people have access to a patient's notes, including secretaries, filing-clerks, nurses, social workers, psychologists and other doctors. It is important that a patient's notes be easily available to a number of people other than the psychotherapist. Perhaps the patient may need to be admitted to hospital; or perhaps someone is carrying out research into the problem of which the patient may be one example. But the patient may feel, with ample justification, that he does not want the details of his sexual life or other intimate matters to be easily available to so many different people, however firmly the necessity of confidentiality has been impressed upon them. This is especially so in small communities in which the patient may be known to members of the hospital staff in a different context.

I think that if the therapist wants to make notes of each therapeutic session, (and he can hardly avoid doing this if his therapy is being supervised, even if he postpones writing anything until the patient has departed) he ought to keep a separate file to which only he has access. He should possess, or have access to, a filing cabinet of which only he possesses the key, so that he can reassure the patient that no-one else can possibly see any notes which he makes during the session. In the ordinary notes, he should record the fact of the patient's attendance, and should also briefly describe his mental state, especially if there appears to have been any considerable change in this, or if the patient appears to be severely depressed. This is simply to provide information in case the patient needs to be admitted to the hospital. The psychotherapist need not record intimate details of the patient's personal life in the ordinary case-notes.

In suggesting this, I am well aware that I am placing an extra burden upon the therapist, and also breaking with hospital tradition. But I am convinced of the necessity of being honest with one's patients; and I entirely sympathise with the anxiety about confidentiality which they often express. When I gave up private practice, I had case-notes of patients ranging over a period of twenty-four years. I hesitated for a long time as to what to do with them. In the end, I decided to burn them all. Since then, I have had a number of enquiries about former patients from other doctors. In the case of patients whom I saw for regular psychotherapy over a long period, I have had no difficulty in answering enquiries provided the patient has given me permission to do so. If one gets to know people really well, one has no problem in remembering them. Only in the case of people I saw diagnostically or for a very few interviews have I had any difficulty in recall.

It is appropriate here to deal with the problem of confidentiality in relation to the patient's general practitioner and other doctors. Many patients in psychotherapy express anxiety about what will be written to their family doctor. Sometimes this is because they have found him imperceptive or unsympathetic toward their emotional problems. Sometimes it is because they fear that letters reaching him will be read by others. Sometimes it is because they know the general practitioner socially, and would be embarrassed to meet him if they felt that he knew their most intimate secrets. In one or two instances, it may emerge that the patient is emotionally involved with the doctor.

I am particularly anxious that general practitioners shall have full information about their patients, and that their experience of emotional problems should be widened. Family doctors ought to be able to deal with a great many of the emotional difficulties with which patients present them and, now that they are getting better teaching in psychiatry, do in fact cope with a wider range of problems than they did when I was a medical student. Nevertheless, if the patient is insistent that the general practitioner shall not be told certain details, that wish must be respected. Sometimes, I show the patient the letter which I am sending to the general practitioner. If any strong objection is vouchsafed, I am generally prepared to amend the letter or to say that, if the patient prefers this, I will speak to his doctor on the telephone rather than put anything in writing. Sometimes I ask permission to tell the general practitioner that there are certain confidential matters which the patient does not want me to reveal to him; especially in instances in which the patient and the doctor have a social, as well as a professional relationship. It is important, though easily forgotten, that the psychotherapist keep the patient's doctor informed about progress, and that a summary of what has been achieved is sent to him when the therapy has come to an end. If the patient wishes to see such a summary, there should be no reason to conceal it from him. In all cases, I try to abide by the principle of being completely honest with the patient.

15

3

Establishing a Pattern

The psychotherapist has seen his new patient for the first time, taken his own history, and arranged a series of subsequent appointments. What does he do next? His next task is to get the patient to talk as freely as possible, whilst he himself stays in the background. This is not as easy as it sounds. Patients who have consulted doctors in the past usually expect them to take the lead, issue instructions, give advice, or ask more questions. Doctors who are not used to practising psychotherapy find it difficult to abandon their traditional authoritarian role. However, the fact that the patient, rather than the doctor, is expected to take the lead in psychotherapeutic interviews is not only the feature of such interviews which most clearly distinguishes them from conventional medical consultations, but also has many important psychological consequences. If I was asked which of Freud's many contributions to the art of psychotherapy was the most significant, I should say that it was his replacement of hypnosis by free association. He took time to reach this. Ernest Jones[1] tells us that Freud did not entirely abandon hypnosis until 1896. In the nineteenth century, hypnosis was fashionable. Moreover, Freud had been influenced by Charcot, whose clinic in Paris he had attended, and also by Bernheim. When Freud and Breuer made their original discovery that hysterical symptoms could often be abolished if the patient could be persuaded to recollect and re-experience the painful emotions connected with the onset of the symptoms, they used hypnosis to facilitate recall, and required the patient to lie upon a couch, whilst the hypnotist sat at its head. When Freud abandoned hypnosis in favour of free association, he retained the couch. This was partly because he did not like being stared at for eight hours per day, and partly because he found that patients could relax and talk more freely if they were lying supine and if the analyst was out of sight.

As originally used, hypnosis was a technique of giving patients positive suggestion. Success in its use principally depended upon the doctor's authority and the patient's compliance. Freud, who was more of an investigator than a therapist, came to dislike a technique which depended upon his authority rather than upon understanding the origins of the symptoms, and which was often unpredictable in its results. Instead, he at first urged his patients to recall the origins of their symptoms whilst in the waking state; and later encouraged still greater autonomy by requiring them to put into words whatever thoughts occurred to them. In Freud's view, 'free association', when honestly undertaken, was bound to lead to the recovery of the memories which the patient appeared to have forgotten.

Today, psychotherapists who use hypnosis are less authoritarian, and generally teach the patient how to enter the hypnotic state himself after some preliminary sessions. Autohypnosis has been extensively used in psychosomatic disorders, and good results claimed in a variety of conditions in which lessening of anxiety and relaxation are therapeutically valuable.[2] Although there is certainly a place for the use of hypnosis and autohypnosis, this book is primarily concerned with the investigative type of psychotherapy based upon analytical techniques. The purpose of analytical psychotherapy is to help the patient to help himself through insight and understanding, and thus to increase his autonomy.

At the second interview, therefore, the psychotherapist ought to abandon the conventional, medical stance which, to a certain extent, must characterise interviews in which a history is being taken, and move on to establish a type of psychotherapeutic session in which the patient takes the lead. Some patients have so much to say that no explanation of what is expected of them is necessary. They plunge in with a monologue which the psychotherapist may find hard to interrupt when he wants to make some comment. Others find great difficulty in exhibiting any kind of spontaneity. This may be because they are so accustomed to treating doctors as authorities that they invariably wait for the great man to speak first; or it may be because, consciously or unconsciously, they resent the situation. It may also be that they are frightened that the psychotherapist is going to uncover things of which they are ashamed; or that he has some magical technique which will give him power over their minds.

If, at a second interview, the patient does not start talking spontaneously, I generally proceed somewhat as follows.

'Last time, I asked you a number of questions about your problems and background. From now on, I want you to take the lead rather than my asking more questions. After all, you are the only person who knows what is going on in your mind. What do *you* feel that you need to talk about?'

If there is no response to this, I may say: 'What were you thinking about on your way to keep this appointment, for instance?'

Patients who are frightened, resentful, or psychologically naive sometimes answer 'Nothing'.

I generally reply: 'I find it very difficult to think of nothing. In fact I believe that's impossible. There are always stray thoughts going through one's head. Perhaps you were having some thoughts about coming to see me again today. Perhaps you had some sort of anticipation about what this second interview was going to be like?'

'I thought you'd ask me some more questions.'

'What kind of questions did you imagine?'

If the patient denies having imagined anything further about the forthcoming interview at this point, and particularly if his manner and tone of voice suggest resentment, I say something like: 'Perhaps you're not feeling like talking to me today. Do you, by any chance feel that you've been pushed into coming? Is there someone else who has said that you *ought* to?'

Patients who are as reluctant to talk as the one I have portrayed have often been overpersuaded by another person to seek psychotherapy; and it may be that their reluctance does not show itself until they are required to do something other than answer direct questions. Most reasonably intelligent patients, even if they are quite uninformed about psychotherapy, very quickly latch on to the idea that what the therapist wants to know is, first, what has been preoccupying them since their last visit, and, second, what is going on in their minds in the here-and-now of the immediate present. If they fail to grasp this, it is reasonable to assume that they are either frightened, or hostile, or both; and one very common reason for hostility is that the patient feels bullied into coming.

This is especially so in the case of the young, though not confined to them. For example, parents often push their adolescents into seeking psychiatric help. As disturbed adolescents are often in rebellion against their parents in any case, they regard the institution of 'treatment' for their problems as another instance of parental lack of understanding, and consequently refuse to talk. Doctors who work in student health services often face the problem that the student with difficulties in his work, or other signs of disturbance, may have been urged to come by his tutor. Even if his relationship with his tutor is a good one, he may still feel his referral to be another manifestation of authoritarian interference.

Very often, such a patient will respond to the psychotherapist's appreciation of the possibility that he is being compelled into coming by someone else by revealing that such is indeed the case. I then generally explain that psychotherapy requires, and is entirely dependent upon, the willing co-operation of the patient, and that if he does not want to discuss his problems further, I certainly shall not press him to do so. Sometimes this way of handling the matter so disposes of the patient's hostility that he becomes immediately co-operative. In other cases, he will decide that he does not want to go into his problems with me, but will deal with them unaided. In such a case, I make a practice of 'leaving the door open' in case he changes his mind. Patients may need time to reflect upon whether they really want to seek help of their own volition.

Inexperienced doctors sometimes make the mistake of dismissing an unco-operative patient as if he was offering them a personal insult instead of trying to appreciate what such a patient may be feeling. When I was a medical student, I

19

remember a consultant physician conducting a teaching 'round' with a group of doctors, nurses, and students of the usual kind. He stopped at the bedside of a patient who evidently disliked being 'taught on' and who asked the physician what he wanted in a manner obviously resentful. Instead of trying to find out *why* the man was resentful, the consultant took umbrage and said: 'Well, if you are going to take that attitude, I'm not going to waste my valuable time investigating your case'. My opinion of that consultant, never very high in any case, dropped still further. Very probably the patient had simply been suffering from that surfeit of being seen by too many unidentifiable doctors, which afflicts many patients in teaching hospitals, or had been overused as a teaching case.

Patients who are frightened are sometimes so extremely tense and anxious that they are unable easily to talk. In such instances, I generally comment on their posture and suggest that they will find it easier to talk if they sit back in the chair and try to relax. Obviously, I also try to discover what is making them frightened. Unsophisticated patients have a variety of anxieties which are often so highly irrational as to raise the supposition that they may be psychotic. They may believe that the therapist has magical powers which enable him to read their thoughts; or that he is going to rob them of control of their own minds by hypnosis, or some other technique. Such patients are generally greatly reassured when the therapist tells them that he is entirely dependent upon their co-operation; that they do not have to tell him anything which they do not wish to reveal; and that he understands that talking to a strange person about one's personal problems can be both difficult and alarming.

Some patients are reluctant to talk because using words to define and clarify problems is unfamiliar to them. This may be because of lack of education; a difficulty which is usually surmountable if the psychotherapist is flexible enough to adapt his use of language to the patient's range. Other patients have been brought up in such a way that they habitually have recourse to action, when faced with difficulties, and do not include 'putting things into words' as action. If, throughout one's life, one has been used to dispelling anger by digging the garden, to alleviating anxiety by taking alcohol, to avoiding confrontation with authority by changing one's job, to 'doing something', however futile or inappropriate, it takes time to learn that clarification through words can be of use. Some such people also believe that any form of self-examination is to be deplored; that introspection is unhealthy, and talking about one's problems self-indulgence. This puritanical attitude is not infrequently found amongst the religious, which, considering that the great religions of the world have generally insisted upon the duty of self-examination, is somewhat surprising. I have generally found that pointing out the kinship between psychotherapy and religious practice dispels the assumption of self-indulgence, a notion which, in any case, tends to disappear when the patient discovers that he has to face things about himself which he may not find easy to accept.

Occasionally, the psychotherapist may have referred to him a patient who turns out to be psychotic. Such patients may exhibit obvious anxiety, but are more likely to be withdrawn and unapproachable. Paranoid schizophrenics, who are, perhaps, the variety of psychotic most likely to be referred in error to the psychotherapist, often have the fears described above as occurring in unsophisticated patients, but in more extreme form. They are also likely to believe that the therapist can insert thoughts into their minds, as part of taking them over. It is very unlikely that such fears will be revealed in the first few sessions; and, if they are revealed, it is more likely that the patient will make accusations rather than admit he is frightened. Thus, I well remember an intelligent young man who was referred to me for the treatment of various phobias. The first few sessions progressed normally enough. Then, quite suddenly, during a pause in our discourse, he said: 'You are trying to hypnotise me, aren't you?' Enquiry revealed a paranoid substructure to his phobic state; he was later admitted to hospital, and, finally, after a number of years of recurrent psychotic breakdowns, committed suicide.

Even the most experienced diagnostician may fail to find evidence of psychosis in a single consultation; especially in highly intelligent patients, who may be expert at hiding their condition. When the inexperienced psychotherapist is faced with such a problem, he will do well to discuss the matter with the consultant who originally saw the patient. Although some psychotic patients need, and to some extent respond to,

SBRLSMD (Whitechapel)

psychotherapy, they are beyond the reach of the beginner. Patients of this kind will be discussed later.

At the beginning of this chapter, I said that the psychotherapist's task is to get the patient to talk as freely as possible whilst himself remaining in the background. I have discussed some of the difficulties which may obstruct this aim; but I would like to emphasise the fact that the majority of patients referred for psychotherapy are eager to talk about their problems, and do not present the therapist with such difficulties.

Reference

1.   Jones, Ernest (1953) *Sigmund Freud: Life and Work.* Vol. 1, p.268. London: Hogarth Press.
2.   Maher-Loughnan, G. P. (1980) 'Clinical applications of hypnosis in medicine'. *Br. J. Hosp. Med.* May pp. 447–55.

4

Making Progress

In this chapter, I shall assume that any initial difficulties in communication have been overcome; that the patient is embarked upon a series of regular visits to the psychotherapist; and that he is able to talk about himself and his problems fairly freely, without having to be urged or persuaded to do so.

Although the process of psychotherapy involves some pain, in that most people find it unpleasant to confront their less admirable aspects, the majority of patients seem to look forward to their visits to the therapist, and discover that putting their difficulties into words is in itself beneficial, even if the therapist says practically nothing.

Why should this be so? What does putting a problem into words involve? If this act of verbalisation is itself helpful, is the presence of a trained psychotherapist really needed? Would not the ear of a sympathetic friend serve the purpose equally well? Or could not the patient confide his difficulties to a diary or a tape-recorder and obtain the same benefit?

I would like to emphasise the fact that, in ordinary social life, there is no equivalent to the psychotherapeutic situation. When uninformed people discuss psychotherapy, they often conceive of the process as boring for the therapist, since their experience of people who talk about themselves is one of tedium. This is partly because, in social life, most people want an exchange, and the person who gives no opportunity for interchange is not playing the expected game and may become irritating. Also, many people who talk about themselves a great deal in social settings *are* boring because their talk is superficial. They may give accounts of their activities, or tell stories about their experiences without revealing anything at all of their inner lives. Indeed, compulsive talkers who tell one 'everything' in minute detail are generally using talk as a method of concealment. If the other person is not allowed to get in a word, there is no danger of genuine interchange. The torrent of talk acts as a kind of smokescreen which prevents the talker from being known. Occasionally such people enter psychotherapy, when it becomes the psychotherapist's task to interrupt the flow and to point out the way in which the patient is using words to conceal and avoid rather than to articulate feeling. Such patients, fortunately, are rare. When people are talking genuinely and sincerely, they are seldom boring. But social life does not afford the opportunity for people who need to do so to talk about themselves at length; and sympathetic friends are usually too anxious to intervene, give advice, or 'do something' to allow the patient to find out enough about himself.

Is the therapist necessary? It is possible, though difficult, to analyse oneself; and modern recording devices could certainly be used to aid the process. Freud, we are told, began his self-analysis in the eighteen-nineties, and continued to set aside the last half-hour of his day for that purpose throughout his life. But few of us are as determined or as honest as Freud. Most people lack the self-discipline needed for regular self-scrutiny. Some require a therapist because they too easily give themselves up in despair: others because they can understand neither themselves nor their fellow-men. Even in those cases in which the minimum of interpretation on the part of the therapist is required, his presence acts as a spur to honesty, as an implicit hope of improvement, as a guarantee that the process of self-exploration is worthwhile. Many of the patients in whom psychotherapy produces valuable results are people who have not thought themselves to be worth bothering with. The therapist's continuing presence and interest is a living proof that at least one person in the world thinks otherwise. Moreover, although insight, in the sense of understanding oneself better, can to some extent be achieved by determined characters who are prepared to record their own thoughts and feelings with scrupulous honesty even when no therapist is with them, self-analysis does not give any opportunity for the operation of one process in the course of psychotherapy which, as we shall see, is of major importance in achieving improvement. This is the progressive change in the patient's relation with the therapist which takes place in every successful psychotherapeutic encounter of any prolonged kind and which will be discussed in a subsequent chapter.

Putting things into words is an act which is less simple than it appears. Indeed, a complete understanding of what is involved would, I believe, involve a knowledge of linguistics and philosophy which I do not possess. The phrase must surely imply that there are mental contents, thoughts, feelings, wishes, problems and so on, which exist in the mind but which have never been clearly formulated. A good deal of the talk which a patient produces during the course of psychotherapy is about things which he knows but which he has never clearly spelled out; things which he may describe as being 'at the back of the mind'. Perhaps the 'tip of the tongue' phenomenon is analogous. One may know that one knows a word without being able quite to recall it. In fact, research has shown that the 'tip of the tongue' phenomenon occurs because the brain does not necessarily store the complete letter sequence of every word which the subject can recognise. The words which we know we know but cannot recall are words which have been incompletely stored and which are therefore incompletely known.

In psychotherapy, many of the things which the patient discovers about himself are things which he may say that he has known all along but never clearly recognised. Such insights, especially when unflattering, may have occurred to him before, but in so fleeting a fashion that they have not been fully registered. Putting things into words, like writing an examination paper, clarifies both what one knows and what one does not know.

Putting things into words also has the effect of giving reality to unformulated mental contents. Thoughts, feelings, phantasies and day-dreams which are not deliberately expressed remain insubstantial. When expressed to another person, they achieve an existence in the world of a more solid kind than is possible if they are only in the subject's head. Putting things into words captures the ephemeral. All of us have thoughts, day-dreams, and feelings which are fleeting, and which like butterflies, disappear if not immediately netted. This is true even of new ideas for which one is searching; so that it is not surprising that it is especially the case with ideas which are unwelcome; discoveries which demonstrate that the subject is less admirable than he had previously supposed.

Many people, when not actively engaged by the world external to them, seem preoccupied with an internal monologue not unlike Molly Bloom's monologue at the end of *Ulysses*. Such a monologue reveals their emotional preoccupations, but is exceedingly difficult to put into words, as anyone who has tried to copy Joyce's extraordinary achievement will find. Nevertheless, the patient in psychotherapy, if both relaxed and honest, will find that he is able to become conscious of many thoughts and feelings which influence his behaviour and attitudes to other people, but which have never been formulated. For example, it is not uncommon to see men whose first thought, on meeting another man, is to wonder about the other's bank balance. Such a patient may be very reluctant to admit that either money or competitiveness plays such a large part in his life until he has put into words the fleeting, quickly suppressed thought which I have given as an example. Many heterosexual men have sexual phantasies about every woman they encounter, but may be quite unaware of this until the psychotherapeutic situation encourages them to express their phantasies in words. The woman who is reported to have said: 'How do I know what I think until I hear what I say?' was posing a question which has relevance for most of us, unless we are writers perpetually engaged in discovering what we think through the act of writing.

Putting things into words has another function. It is the means whereby we detach ourselves both from the world about us and from the inner world of our own emotions and thoughts. It is by means of words that we objectify, that we are enabled to stand back from our own experience and reflect upon it. Words about the self make possible a psychical distance from the self, and, without distance, neither understanding nor control, nor willed, deliberate change is possible. It is true that when one embarks upon self-observation, one enters upon an infinite regress. I may observe myself, but I cannot observe the 'I' which is the observer; or, if I succeed in doing that, am precluded from observing the 'I' which observes the 'I' which observes . . . and so ad infinitum. But the fact that we can never observe the whole of ourselves need not prevent us from scrutinising what we can with accuracy. I may not be able to see my own back; but I can get a good idea of it with the help of a mirror, or by comparison with someone like myself.

The act of verbalisation makes possible critical appraisal. If one can talk about an emotion, one is, at least at that moment, no longer possessed by it. To say 'That is what I am feeling' is to be separated, however slightly, from that feeling. Instead of being at the mercy of an emotion, one begins to achieve some power over it. This does not mean that, by putting an emotion into words, one rids oneself of it; nor would one necessarily want to do so. But the act of talking *about* something which one is feeling, rather than simply feeling, is the first step toward control.

That is why it is helpful to put into words even aspects of the self which cannot be altered. Recognition of 'That is how I really am' creates a new order in the mind in which reality takes the place of phantasy. Suppose, for example, that a man who has hitherto thought himself to be particularly kind and peace-loving discovers that he has an aggressive side to his character which he has never previously admitted. The discovery may not banish his aggression; but it will tend to modify his expression of it because the process of becoming conscious of a tendency brings it more within the range of control. People who are unconscious of how aggressive they are are often over-critical 'without meaning to be'; are too severe with their children, make hurtful asides, or denigratory jokes. When such people become fully aware of the aggressive side of their nature, such unintended manifestations of it tend to diminish.

Those who are both intelligent and honest may therefore gain a good deal from talking about themselves and their problems at length, even if the psychotherapist makes only minimal interventions. This must be a comforting reflection for the inexperienced psychotherapist, who may feel that he does not know enough to make confident interpretations. He may rest assured that, provided the patient has reached the stage at which he can talk about himself honestly, he is doing something valuable by simply being there and providing the situation in which such talk is possible. As I pointed out earlier, there is no equivalent in social life to the situation which obtains in psychotherapy. I have already written about encouraging the patient to take the lead at each session. It is also important that the therapist refrain from giving advice, although he may not be able to avoid doing this entirely. Jung once said: 'Good advice is often a doubtful remedy but generally not dangerous since it has so little effect.' There are two main reasons why the psychotherapist should avoid giving direct advice as far as possible. The first is that, in dealing with patients who are seeking psychotherapy, he is often trying to help them with problems to which there are no definitive answers. If you go to a doctor with a pain and he says, 'You have appendicitis; this is what you should do', that is perfectly reasonable. But if you go to a psychotherapist and you are in doubt as to whether or not you should get married, or you want to know how you should bring up a child, or whether to take a particular job, or how to treat your aged mother, you are asking questions to which there are no hard and fast answers, and which may involve moral considerations about which there might be considerable disagreement. What the psychotherapist has to do is to help the patient to make up his own mind by facilitating the patient's discovery of what he himself thinks and feels. The second reason for avoiding giving advice is that although patients who are uncertain of themselves often ask for advice, it does not aid their development toward independence to give it to them. Of course we all need advice in fields in which we are not expert. We need lawyers, accountants, electricians, plumbers and hosts of other experts whom we consult as need arises; and we are generally content to accept their expert advice in technical matters of which we know little or nothing. But giving advice in matters which are not merely technical is likely to seem patronising, and thus to be denigrating to the patient. The problems which a patient brings to a psychotherapist are problems in living which we all have to face and which cannot be studied and mastered in the way in which electrical circuits or accountancy or law can be studied and mastered. Living is not an esoteric subject; and no-one is an expert at it. The psychotherapist is no more an expert at living than anyone else.

What he should be expert in is in making relationships with people, in understanding them, and in facilitating their development in a psychotherapeutic situation is such a way that they become more confident in dealing with their own problems in living. His reluctance to give advice is itself therapeutic, in that it carries the implication that, once his problems are more clearly understood, the patient will be as capable as anyone else of making his own decisions.

5

Interpretation

When I was in training as a psychiatrist, one of my teachers, Emanuel Miller, used to tell the story that he once saw a patient over a period of about a year. The man came three times a week, took up his place on the analytic couch, and, at every session, plunged straight into 'free association'. At the end of the year, the patient pronounced himself cured and offered his deepest thanks to Dr Miller. The latter asserted that, during the whole of this period, he himself said nothing whatever. Although it is possible that Dr Miller may have slightly underestimated his own verbal participation, this story is not as incredible as it generally appears to the uninitiated. The inexperienced psychotherapist is not only anxious about what he should say to a patient, but also usually talks too much. In ordinary social interchange, we seldom tolerate silence for long and, if we cannot think of anything interesting to say, take refuge in banalities about the weather. Psychotherapists must become accustomed to tolerating periods of silence. These may indicate that there is something which the patient is reluctant to talk about, or that he is finding it difficult to put into words thoughts and feelings which he may never previously have explored. When a patient who has previously been talking freely becomes 'stuck', it is legitimate for the therapist to take up and repeat the end of the patient's last sentence with an interrogatory tone which suggests that he knows that there is more to come and that he is anxious to hear what that more may be.

Patient: 'And then I changed schools.....' (pause).

Therapist: 'You changed schools?'

Patient: 'Yes... I changed schools.....' (long pause).

Therapist: (after appropriate long wait) 'It sounds as if you may be recalling something about that change which is important or difficult to talk about?'

Patient: 'That's true. I don't know why, but I found myself thinking about a particular boy... He used to make models in plasticine. One day he made a little figure of a man, and stuck on it a penis. It made the other boys laugh, but I was very embarrassed.'

Therapist: 'You still are embarrassed, I think, and that is perhaps why you paused for so long.'

This last sentence of the therapist might, I suppose, be called an interpretation, though that is to give a big name to a trivial and obvious instance of making sense of the patient's difficulty in talking.

Making interpretations is part of the therapist's task; some would say his most important task; but the phrase has acquired a grandiose ring which is sometimes taken to imply that only those who have been initiated into the esoteric mysteries of the unconscious are entitled to embark upon it. Psychoanalytic interpretations may, in some instances, be based upon knowledge of, or assumptions about, psychopathology which are familiar to the experienced psychotherapist but which may be obscure to the uninitiated. For example, Kleinian interpretations about 'internal objects', or Jungian interpretations about 'animus' and 'anima' will probably be totally incomprehensible to the therapist in training who is just embarking upon his first psychotherapeutic case, and who has not yet had time or inclination to read much analytic literature. Let him take comfort from the fact that such interpretations will also be incomprehensible to the kind of patient he is likely to be seeing as a novice; and, even if true, would have to be rephrased by the therapist making them if they were to have any meaning for the patient. Therapists who know each other, especially if they belong to the same 'school', tend to use jargon as a kind of shorthand in talking between themselves, just as do specialists in any field from insurance to nuclear physics. This is sometimes unnerving to the beginner, and has the effect (not entirely unintended) of making him feel himself to be an outsider and inferior. If teachers of psychotherapy start using incomprehensible jargon to their pupils, I recommend that the latter should challenge them to say exactly what they mean in straightforward language. Unless the teacher is dealing with a sophisticated analytic patient who has been in treatment for some time and who therefore knows the jargon, he will have to couch his interpretations in ordinary language in any case. Jargon may be convenient shorthand, but is as often misused to lend a spurious air of profundity to utterances which are nothing of the kind.

The kind of interpretations which anyone can make in psychotherapy after only a short period of training can, I think, be divided into three main varieties. First, it is often the therapist's task to make the incomprehensible comprehensible. Most patients seeking psychotherapy suffer from symptoms which do not make sense to them, and which therefore seem more menacing than they need. To be afflicted with agoraphobia, or obsessional thoughts of violence, or an unacceptably 'perverse' sexual preoccupation makes a patient feel that his mind is less under control than that of people he conceives to be 'normal'; that he therefore may be 'mad' or becoming so; or that, if not actually mad, he is peculiarly afflicted. To find that such symptoms are familiar to the psychotherapist, and cause him no particular alarm, is itself a relief; and further relief follows if the therapist is able to provide some seemingly reasonable explanation of their origin. Thus, in the course of only a few interviews, the therapist might be able to make 'interpretations' about a patient's agoraphobia.

'It sounds, from what you say, as if, when you were a small child, your mother was so anxious about your venturing out alone that she made the world seem a frightening place for you. If such a fear occurs in a child of three, we think nothing of it, because most children of three gain more confidence as they get older, and can venture further and further independently. The only abnormal thing about your fear is that it has persisted.'

There are, of course, other contributory factors to agoraphobia, and other explanations of its origin; but even so simple and obvious an explanation as the one given above not only relieves some of the patient's fear of the incomprehensible but is also true so far as it goes; that is, if from what the patient has said, it does genuinely appear that, as a small child, he was over-protected.

Similarly, interpretation of a patient's obsessional thoughts of violence can often be both correct and along relatively simple lines, at least as a start. A woman once came to see me with the complaint that she had an intrusive fear that she might boil her new-born baby in one of those copper vessels which used to be used for boiling dirty washing. Her history revealed that she was very much under the domination of her mother-in-law, in whose house she was staying; and that she had allowed the mother-in-law, much against her own will, to take over far too much of the management of her new-born baby. Her husband was also frightened of his mother and reluctant to stand up for his wife's rights against her. It was against this background that the obsessional thought of boiling the baby occurred. An interpretation along the lines that, if the baby was out of the way, many of her problems with regard both to her husband and to his mother would disappear, and that it was therefore not 'unnatural' that the idea of disposing of the baby should have occurred to her, brought her considerable relief. She had to accept that she was not as 'nice' as she had supposed; and that her exaggerated submissiveness was not a fruitful way of relating with relatives, and this made sense to her. The therapist's knowledge that it is just to such submissive people that the most violent obsessional thoughts occur no doubt contributed to the patient's relief in that a therapist takes such things for granted. The inexperienced therapist who has never encountered such a case before will not have this confidence, but will soon acquire it if he sees enough patients.

Thus, one function of interpretation is to make the incomprehensible comprehensible. This seldom immediately abolishes any neurotic symptom, but it does have the effect of relieving any anxiety which the patient may have about his sanity; and also converts the symptom from a shadowy, unknown adversary into a more clearly identified problem which can be worked at. Thus, the agoraphobic begins to tackle the whole area of dependency; whilst the obsessional sees that, if she could begin to stand up for herself more in all kinds of situations, she would not be plagued with compulsive thoughts of violence.

Interpretation is also concerned with tracing connections between events, symptoms, and personality characteristics which are not immediately obvious. Different schools of psychotherapy differ in the importance which they attribute to the events of early childhood as determinants of later personality and problems, but most would agree that the child is father to the man, whether or not they consider that the child is formed chiefly by genetic, or chiefly by parental, influence. Making sense out of neurotic symptoms may or may not include reference to the patient's childhood. In the example of the agoraphobic it did; in the example of the obsessional thought of violence it did not. But both interpretations are of course incomplete. Perhaps a complete interpretation of any personal trait or symptom is impossible. When one embarks upon understanding a symptom, one does not know how far this may lead. Why was the obsessional patient so submissive? Had she had parents of whom she was frightened; or had she been brought up in the kind of Christian household in which turning the other cheek was the only legitimate response? A single symptom is like a stone causing ripples in the pond of the personality, of which the 'cause' may have long since sunk beneath the surface, but which leaves traces which spread out indefinitely.

Many behaviour patterns which were adopted in childhood may have been appropriate at the time, or indeed the only possible forms of adaptation. But some persist inappropriately into adult life, whether from inertia or for other reasons. Interpretation can reveal this persistence, and thus help the patient to begin to experiment with other ways of behaving. Patients who have been 'strictly' brought up, overdominated by parents, for example, may, out of habit, persist in being obedient followers in situations in which leadership is demanded of them. Moreover, they may rationalise their lack of initiative in terms of consideration for other people's opinions when the truth is that they are still behaving like frightened children. Understanding one's own behaviour in this kind of way is sometimes called 'insight', a term to which we shall return in subsequent chapters.

A third function of interpretation is to point out discrepancies between what a patient says that he feels, and what his description of his behaviour indicates that he actually does feel. Thus, if a patient says that he is very fond of his wife, but habitually neglects her wishes, forgets what she tells him, or disparages her in front of others, it is obvious that there is a discrepancy between what the patient says that he feels toward her and what his behaviour indicates that he feels. Not all interpretations of such discrepancies are negative, in the sense of revealing harsh truths about himself which the patient is avoiding. Many patients entering psychotherapy undervalue themselves, and are nicer or more intelligent than they perceive themselves to be. Thus, a timid patient may be bolder than he gives himself credit for; or a patient concerned about hostile feelings be kinder than he realises. If one reads Freud, one is apt to come away with the idea that all interpretation is bound to be of the kind which reveals unpleasant aspects of character which the patient has failed to recognise in himself. This is not the case. Although we are all apt to deceive ourselves, we do so in both directions; in overestimation of our bad qualities as well as of our virtues.

Interpretations should never be dogmatically phrased or delivered in an authoritarian tone. There is no point in making interpretations which do not win the patient's assent or make sense to him. Moreover, the therapist may be wrong in what he surmises. I generally preface any interpretation which I make with some such tentative beginning as: 'It sounds rather as if you . . .' If the patient finds my suggested interpretation illuminating, the fact that I have phrased it undogmatically will not diminish its effect: whilst, if he does not agree, my lack of dogmatism makes it easier for him to say so.

Interpretation is a term which carries with it the implication of a special expertise in penetrating the patient's self-deception. Analysts are conceived of as persons whose function is to penetrate beyond appearances, who never take anything at face value, who read a hidden significance into the most trivial utterance. Of course there is a sense in which this can be true, in that prolonged practice in observation of others does lead to psychotherapists making connections between overt utterance and underlying preoccupations which are not obvious to those who are unused to thinking in this way. But great novelists, like Proust, are at least as observant. This is not to say that interpretation should or need be a kind of translation; an idea which must surely take origin from Freud's idea that dreams were invariably concealments; the 'manifest content' being what the patient remembered, what appeared on the surface; and the 'latent content' the 'true' meaning only to be revealed by the interpretations of the analyst.

The assumption that overt utterances are invariably masking something hidden and less acceptable has led psychoanalysts into making interpretations which are absurd. For example, in R. D. Laing's[1] book about his children, *Conversations with Adam and Natasha* he records Natasha asking the question 'Can God kill himself?' One of Laing's friends who is called Monty, and who is also presumably an analyst, is told of this question of Natasha's. His comment is as follows. 'There is an incredibly close relationship between sex and death. I will tell you what the question is saying. She is asking "Does God masturbate?"' Laing responds; 'And that is "Does daddy masturbate"' Monty goes on: 'Precisely. She wishes to know whether she can do it with you instead of mummy.' Does Natasha really wish to know any such thing? There seems to me no evidence whatever to suggest it. Laing records that his children were brought up to believe in God and to say their prayers. Monty's assumption that Natasha's question refers to her father when she speaks of God underestimates both her intelligence and the circumstances of her upbringing; and, whilst there are psychological connections between the experience of orgasm (the 'little death') and the idea of death, there is no reason to suppose that Natasha was confusing the two when she raises what, if she believes in God, is actually an interesting problem.

Psychoanalytic literature abounds with interpretations which are no less absurd. In his learned book on Leonardo, for example, K. R. Eissler[2] confidently asserts that Leonardo's interest in drawing and shifting patterns made by water took origin from his having wet his bed in early childhood. There is no evidence that Leonardo was in fact enuretic; nor do we know what was the contemporary attitude to bed wetting in fifteenth-century Italy.

Such interpretations derive from two psychoanalytic

assumptions. The first is that anything which deeply engages human interest must derive from primitive bodily sources. The second is that primitive bodily satisfactions are so unacceptable that they are invariably concealed by various mental man-oeuvres such as sublimation. Take, for example, Ernest Jones'[3] statement about the arts in his chapter on that subject in his life of Freud. 'When one considers the material used in the five arts — paint, clay, stone, words, and sounds — any psychologist must conclude that the passionate interest in bringing an order-liness out of the chaos must signify at the same time an extraor-dinary sublimation of the most primitive infantile enjoyments and the most extreme denial of them.' It is true that many neurotic symptoms conceal primitive drives which are unac-ceptable. But it does not follow that every utterance, every interest, or every piece of behaviour is not what it seems or is a concealment. It is not even true of dreams, as Freud supposed. Although dreams may certainly require interpretation if we are to understand them, this is because they are couched in sym-bolic and pictorial 'language' rather than in words. Some dreams are certainly concerned with matters which the dreamer finds unacceptable or difficult to manage, but the difficulty in understanding them does not occur because of concealment. Many dreams contain overtly aggressive and sexual imagery without any attempt at concealment.

It should be remembered that, at the time Freud was writing, concealment was much more in evidence than it is today. Indeed, it is largely on account of Freud's work that we are much more prepared than were the inhabitants of *fin-de-siècle* Vienna to accept that we all have aggressive and sexual impulses of a crude kind. It should also be recalled that Freud's early patients seem mostly to have been hysterical women, suffering from rather gross forms of both amnesic and conversion hys-teria of a kind which, today, are seldom encountered. These are the kind of patients who, more than any other, tend to conceal their true nature from themselves. Hysterics are experts in self-deception in a way not shared by other types of personality, which is why they sometimes seem irritatingly histrionic and false in their interaction with others. I think that Freud's exciting discovery that piercing the veil of concealment could often abolish hysterical symptoms led him to lay too much emphasis upon concealment in other types of neurotic disorder, and to the assumption that interpretation must always aim at undoing such concealment. In clinical practice, interpretation is much more often concerned with drawing attention to discrepancies, with pointing out unrecognised connections, and with making sense out of the apparently incomprehensible than with the stripping off of masks. The latter process may come into it, but is not the main object.

Making sense of the patient's symptoms and discourse must of course depend upon certain assumptions about life and the nature of human beings which are held by the therapist. No-one can escape from the influence of the current beliefs of his time and culture; and no doubt future generations, better informed than we are about psychology and biology, will scoff at some of the interpretations we offer our patients today. Moreover, theoretical disagreements between the various analytical schools undoubtedly influence the type of explanatory interpretation which is offered. Thus, the Kleinian, whose understanding of human beings rests upon the assumed vicissitudes of the infant at the breast, will endeavour to trace the origin of symptoms to that phase of the infant's development.

The Jungian analyst will be alert to detect compensatory patterns and evidence of archetypal phenomena; whilst the Adlerian will be predisposed to find evidence of 'striving for superiority' and the like. The doctor beginning psychotherapy may be put off by discovering that there is apparently no one 'truth' to which every psychotherapist subscribes.

This does not matter nearly so much as the novice supposes. There are several reasons for this. First, there is general agreement amongst psychotherapists about many more areas of psychopathology than is usually realised. My own training was originally Jungian; and I later had some experience of analysis from a Freudian; but I have had no difficulty in communicating with analysts of other persuasions, or in reaching agreement as to the nature of a particular patient's problems. Many of the difficulties in communications which do arise are semantic. Thus, there are analogies to be found between Jung's notion of archetypes and Melanie Klein's 'internal objects'. Jung[4] himself gives examples of cases which can be interpreted with equal validity from either a Freudian or Adlerian point of view. 'With

Adler the emphasis is placed upon a subject who, no matter what the object, seeks his own security and supremacy; with Freud the emphasis is placed wholly upon objects, which, according to their specific character, either promote or hinder the subject's desire for pleasure.' However, if we were to confine ourselves to giving explanations of specific neurotic symptoms in terms of their meaning, rather than of their origin, we should find that there was a considerable measure of agreement. I believe that all psychotherapists would agree, for example, that schizoid patients experience a most difficult dilemma in that, if they allow themselves to get close to people, this is somehow dangerous; whilst if they remain remote, they experience intolerable isolation. The origin of this dilemma might be in dispute. Some would maintain that the patient was more frightened of the harm he might do to other people than of the damage that they might inflict on him. But all would agree that both types of fear enter into the patient's search for safety from involvement.

There are many analogies to be found between psychoanalytic theory and learning theory. Even so esoteric a conception as the formation of internal objects by introjection can be put in other ways which relate the idea to what is generally agreed. Children are often said to 'assimilate their parents' standards' which then, presumably, reside somewhere within their psyche, but which may, in due course be discarded or got rid of if the child comes to disagree with them. The fact that Kleinians would use language referring to bodily processes of swallowing and excretion reflects the belief that some analysts have that when they are using body language they are on firm ground; whereas of course all language, including body language, is symbolic, and much is metaphorical.

Nearly all the differences in interpretation of the same phenomena as exhibited by neurotic patients are resolvable; and those that are not are, I think, touching a different level of discourse in which the 'religious' aspects of the differences between the different schools are touched upon. Beliefs as to which is the worst type of trauma, for example, have influenced analysts of different theoretical backgrounds without, I suspect, making much difference to their results or even to what they say to the patient. Rycroft[5] lists sexual seduction by adults, the trauma of birth, the discovery of the difference between the sexes, separation from the mother in infancy, and fear of being overwhelmed by one's own impulses as possible 'causes' of neurosis, which have been differently emphasised by different analysts.

The sceptical might argue that any interpretation is better than none; and that so long as the patient 'believes in' his analyst, he will swallow any interpretation which is offered, whether it is in terms of supposed vicissitudes at the breast or whether in terms of the activities of malign little men from outer space. There is some truth in this, but not so much as is generally supposed. In practice, questions of origin turn out to be much less important than the existential question of what the patient is actually doing in the here and now. Whether, for example, one believes that obsessionality does or does not take origin from overstrict toilet training is a theoretical problem of very little importance. In fact, this is one of the Freudian theories which the evidence does not seem to support. What does matter is that the therapist understands how obsessionals behave and feel; what their rituals mean to them; why they have compulsive thoughts; and why their lives are based on taking precautions. Obviously, much adult obsessional behaviour can be related to parental influence, and taking a proper history of the patient's childhood development will provide the therapist with plenty of examples of parents' over-anxiety, scrupulousness, fear of dirt and contamination and so on. But this material is best used to make a coherent story about how the patient's adult personality is related to his childhood personality and training; and a coherent story is what is needed to make sense out of the patient's symptoms and present adaptation to life. No such story is ever complete; and the therapist can never fully determine how much of patient's adult personality is the result of early damage and how much to indefinable genetic causes.

Whether a patient's obsessionality is genetic in origin, or due to strict training, is unimportant for the purposes of therapy. Intellectually precocious children are often oversensitive to hints dropped by parents, and therefore react to the parents as if they were more authoritarian than they were in fact. There are cases in which one cannot help but be convinced, however sceptical, that something went wrong with the infant's relation with his mother at a very early age; and it is interesting that modern research is tending to confirm the suppositions of analysts, in that infants are being discovered to be far more responsive to their surroundings, auditorily, visually, and through touch than has hitherto been supposed, and also that they are more in need of stimulation — being talked to, played with, and so on — than had been realised. But what matters is not that the therapist convinces the patient that this or that type of traumatic upbringing is *the* cause of his symptoms, about which, as I have indicated, there might be various theoretical differences of opinion, but that he understands what the patient is, and what he has experienced in the course of his development.

Doctrinaire analysts who have not made adequate rapport with their patients, and who only understand human nature in terms of a rigid doctrinal scheme rather than by means of their own intuitive understanding of both themselves and other human beings sometimes alienate their patients by giving interpretations couched in jargon. An example of total failure of communication between patient and analyst can be found in the psychologist Professor Sutherland's[6] book about his own neurotic difficulties, *Breakdown*. No wonder Sutherland was confirmed in his belief that analysis was no good; that is, if one accepts his account as anywhere near accurate. Such analysts have substituted belief for understanding and turned their therapy into a process of conversion rather than a means of intimately getting to know another human being. Some writers, like William Sargant, obsessed with 'brainwashing', have supposed that all the psychodynamic psychotherapies depend upon conversion for such cures as they achieve. This, I am sure, is inaccurate. What does help people is a mixture of factors which we shall discuss in the course of this book, but it is a mixture of which conversion is not the prime ingredient. I doubt if many of my patients knew whether I was a Jungian or a Freudian or indeed belonged to any 'school'. I am sure I never converted anybody into being a Jungian or a Freudian; and yet I think the results that I achieved, modest though they were, probably stand comparison with those of others.

There are certain categories of neurotic behaviour and experience which the student can learn about from books, lectures, seminars and the clinical experience of taking histories from patients in outpatients. But he will learn more from taking on a few patients for prolonged psychotherapy whom he gets to know really well; and from exploration of his own problems and defences. The first essential for being a good psychotherapist is not a foolproof theoretical scheme, but a wide capacity for empathy with a variety of personality types.

References
1. Laing, R. D. (1977) *Conversations with Adam and Natasha*. New York: Pantheon Books.
2. Eissler, K. R. (1962) *Leonardo da Vinci: Psychoanalytic Notes on the Enigma*. London: Hogarth Press and Institute of Psycho-Analysis.
3. Jones, Ernest (1957) *Sigmund Freud: Life and Work*. Vol. III, p. 445. London: Hogarth Press.
4. Jung, C. G. (1942) *Two Essays on Analytical Psychology*. Collected Works, Volume 7, p. 41. London: Routledge and Kegan Paul (1953).
5. Rycroft, Charles (1968) *Anxiety and Neurosis*, p. 29. London: Allen Lane, The Penguin Press.
6. Sutherland, Stuart (1976) *Breakdown*. London: Weidenfeld and Nicolson.

6

Dreams, Daydreams, Paintings, Writings

In the course of his work with patients, the psychotherapist must be prepared to listen to, and comment upon, dreams. Since the interpretation of dreams still tends to be regarded as an esoteric skill possessed only by those with long experience and a full analytic training, beginners often shy away from dreams as being beyond their competence. This is a pity; for although not all dreams are revealing or helpful in therapy, some are both; and if the therapist is not prepared to tackle them, he may be depriving himself and the patient of something valuable.

Should the patient be asked for dreams? Some therapists, who adhere closely to the rule that the patient should always take the lead without prompting, say that one should never interfere with the patient's spontaneity by such an enquiry. Others, of whom I am one, think that it is legitimate to ask whether the patient has dreams he would like to discuss, provided that the question is not interrupting the patient's flow of talk or distracting him from some urgent emotional problem with which he is trying to wrestle.

In Chapter 2, I suggested that the psychotherapist who has a new patient referred to him would be well advised to take his own history. This is a good moment to establish whether the patient is the kind of person who remembers his dreams or who attaches any significance to them. The anxiety which accompanies going to see a new doctor for the first time often seems to provoke dreams which are remembered, and it is always worth asking a new patient first, whether he has many dreams which he remembers, and, second, whether he had a dream on the night before he came to see the therapist for the first time. If, for example, the patient has dreamed that he was setting out on a journey, became very anxious because he thought he was going to miss a train, and finally arrived at his destination only to find that a station-master or policeman was waiting for him with an impatient frown, his attitude to authority in the shape of the therapist will be immediately obvious, and will provide a valuable and instantly revealing topic for discussion.

During the initial taking of a history, it is also well worth while enquiring whether the patient had nightmares as a child; and especially if he had recurrent dreams during childhood. Recurrent dreams seem often to be statements about unsolved problems; and may, in a short space, epitomise a whole series of difficulties which can, as it were, be subsumed under one heading. For example, one man recalled that, as a small boy, he had had a recurrent, extremely unpleasant, dream in which he was striving, unsuccessfully, to unravel a complicated network in which pieces of string or wool formed an interlacing pattern of an irregular kind in which the threads were inextricably tangled. The dream induced a feeling of impotent helplessness, in which the dreamer felt that no effort on his part could ever be effective in unravelling the knots. Such a dream can be 'interpreted' on different levels; and would no doubt be given different meanings by analysts of different schools. In my submission, it needs no interpretation at all, but can be taken as a valuable point of departure for enquiring into the patient's childhood. Did he often feel helpless in the way that the dream indicates? If so, why had he become so discouraged? Did this feeling of helplessness apply to life in general, or only to particular aspects of his childhood strivings? Does he ever feel like this today? Such a recurrent dream usually leaves behind a vivid affective memory; and its emotional tone, recalled as the patient recounts it, at once opens a window into the inner world of the patient's feelings.

It is also valuable to ask for dreams on those occasions upon which the patient who is in regular treatment comes to a session and announces that he has 'nothing to say'. Very often a dream recalled in such circumstances contains some indication of the problem which is blocking the flow of the patient's thoughts and discourse. Perhaps it is some intimate fact about himself which he has been too ashamed to reveal. Perhaps it is something which he has felt toward the therapist but which he has not realised or been able to admit. Dreams are often useful as ways of indirectly circumventing an impasse. There is, at the time of writing, no generally accepted theory as to the meaning of dreams; but this need not deter us from making practical use of them. It was Freud who, in modern times, was responsible for reviving the idea that dreams were worth taking seriously; and although his original views on dreams have not been confirmed, we owe him a debt for having re-established their importance. Freud believed that dreams represented unfulfilled, and often unacceptable, wishes, most of which referred to instinctual impulses originating in the dreamer's early childhood. ' . . .we are justified in saying that almost every civilised man retains the infantile forms of sexual life in some respect or other. We can thus understand how it is that repressed infantile sexual wishes provide the most frequent and strongest motive-forces for the construction of dreams.'[1] Such wishes, he believed, did not appear directly in dreams, but were disguised in various ways in order to make them acceptable to the dreamer. Hence the dream required 'interpretation'. What the dreamer himself recalled was only the 'manifest content'; the 'latent content', the true meaning of the dream, could only be discerned after a lengthy process in which the dreamer's associations to all the images in the dream had been subjected to trained analytical scrutiny.

Although dreams are not couched in the language of everyday speech, there is really no evidence that all dreams are concealing something unacceptable. Nor is there sufficient reason to believe that all dreams represent unfulfilled wishes. Freud himself recognised this when considering the dreams of persons who have been subjected to some 'traumatic' incident, and who have recurrent dreams in which the incident occurs undisguised. He postulated that this phenomenon might indicate that the dream was an attempt at mastering a disturbing stimulus; a way of looking at dreams which I think is more fruitful than his original theory.

Jung took a very different view of dreams from that advanced by Freud. First, he did not consider that dreams were concealments, but rather that they were expressed in a symbolic language which might, or might not, be difficult to understand, but which was, in essence, a natural form of human expression. Poetry, for example, is another kind of human utterance in which metaphor and symbol play a predominant role; but we do not think of most poetry as wilfully obscure on that account. Second, Jung believed that all kinds of things could be found in dreams. 'The view that dreams are merely the imaginary fulfilments of repressed wishes is hopelessly out of date. There are, it is true, dreams which manifestly represent wishes or fears; but what about all the other things? Dreams may contain ineluctable truths, philosophical pronouncements, illusions, wild phantasies, memories, plans, anticipations, irrational experiences, even telepathic visions, and heaven knows what besides.'[2] Third, Jung supposed that the psyche was a self-regulating system in the same way as the body is a self-regulating system; this is discussed in my book on Jung.[3] The conscious and unconscious parts of the mind are conceived as being in reciprocal relation with one another. It follows from this idea that dreams, considered as emanating from the unconscious, can, in some instances, be considered as compensating for some conscious attitude of mind which is one-sided or extreme. In my book on Jung I quoted the dream of a girl who saw her mother as a hostile and destructive figure in a dream, although, in conscious life, she had nothing but good to say of her. Jung quotes instances in which men who had overestimated their own powers consciously had dreams indicating that their limits had actually been reached.

When patients report dreams, it is helpful to bear in mind three possible ways of looking at them. First, some dreams certainly can represent wishes, very often of a sexual or ambitious kind, just as do daydreams. Second, dreams often seem to serve as an outlet for impulses which have been impossible to express, or which are partially unrecognised by the dreamer. Aggressive impulses toward the therapist or toward employers, parents and other authorities are frequent contents of dreams. So are sexual impulses toward people whom the dreamer desires but who, for social or other reasons, are inaccessible to him. Homosexual dreams may occur in those who are predominantly heterosexual; heterosexual dreams occur in homosexuals. Third, dreams do often have a compensatory aspect, as in the cases described by Jung. Consciousness strives toward making our views simple and clear-cut; but there is nearly always another side to any conscious attitude we may profess. Thus, dreams frequently bring out some feeling of liking towards people we had thought we wholly disliked, or vice versa. The atheist may discover a religious side to himself; or the scientist that he is not as rational as he had supposed.

Fourth, dreams *do* often relate to problems with which the dreamer is struggling, but which he has not yet resolved. If we are faced with a social situation of which we are nervous, we commonly rehearse our behaviour; imagine what the occasion will be like; think of what we might say or how we might appear, and, in general, try to reduce our anxiety by being forearmed for any eventuality that we can foresee. Dreams often seem to bring up problems of which the patient may be only half aware, but to which he is trying to apply anticipatory processing of the kind I am describing. This problem-solving aspect of dreaming is illustrated by those dreams of scientists and other creative people in which solutions are found; although it is fair to say that answers to problems are more often encountered in states of reverie, half-way between sleep and waking; that is, in day-dreams rather than in night dreams.

When patients report dreams, the meaning of the dream may at once be obvious to either therapist or patient, or to both. On the other hand, it may be entirely obscure. In the latter case, I ask the patient to tell me what comes to mind about the various images in the dream, and in this way usually manage to get some rather general idea of what the dream is about. Although some dreams bring back the past and are certainly derivatives of the patient's early childhood, others are much more directly related to the events of the day; more particularly, it seems to me, to events of which the significance has not been fully appreciated by the dreamer, or which have presented problems to him which he has not entirely been able to deal with. Psychotherapists in training tend to feel alarmed if their patient produces a dream, since they think that the patient will expect them to give an exact, complete interpretation of it. In practice,

47

this seldom, if ever, happens. Patients soon realise that dreams are not material which allows of dogmatic interpretation, but that they are often valuable indicators pointing toward emotional preoccupations to which, perhaps, the patient had not attached sufficient value. Moreover, the patient is asked to contribute as much toward the understanding of the dream as is the therapist, or ought to be so asked. That is, he is requested to give his associations to the various images and incidents in the dream, and so shares responsibility in the attempt to reach an acceptable and convincing interpretation. Some dreams are easily understood, and either illumine the dreamer's past, or else shed light upon his present problems. Others cannot be understood at the time, but may become comprehensible at a later stage in treatment in the light of further discoveries. Occasionally dreams provide both patient and therapist with experiences of unforgettable depth. These are the 'collective' dreams beloved by Jung and his followers which seem to come from a remote source, beyond anything which the dreamer himself could have consciously imagined. It is often possible to detect mythological themes in such dreams of the kind encountered in fairy stories and folk-lore. Jung believed, and I share his conviction, that there is a mythological substratum to human experience of which we are not normally aware, but which manifests itself in various ways not necessarily recognised as such. The enormous popularity of Tolkien's *Lord of the Rings* bears witness to man's hunger for myth and allegory; a need which may also be partially met by some varieties of science fiction. When we become caught up in a world of heroic adventure, in which battles are fought between good and evil forces, great deeds accomplished, kingdoms won and lost, sacrifices demanded, high courage manifested, our lives take on a significance not to be found in the common round of getting and spending. It seems to me likely that some such feeling of participating in great events may be necessary for psychic health; an idea borne out by the decrease of neurotic illness in wartime: but to pursue this idea is not only out of place in this context, but would require another book. It must suffice to indicate that dreams do sometimes provide entry to an inner world of mythological type; and that both therapist and patient may find themselves impressed and enthralled by such dreams.

There are many examples of this kind of dream to be found in the works of Jung and his followers.

Years ago, a patient told me the following dream. I quote it, not because it is an example of a mythological dream, although it has obvious connections with the world of myth, but because it illustrates the fact that study of a single dream can raise a great number of questions about the dreamer's life which are worth exploring.

A man dreamed that he was looking into the window of a shop. Inside was a statuette of a beautiful woman standing upon a square base. Since both the statuette and its base were made of some translucent material, the dreamer could see that there were letters carved upon the underside of the base. He knew that what was written there was the secret of life. But, because the letters were, from his viewpoint, upside down and the wrong way round, he could not read them.

The dream raises many questions. What is the dreamer's relation with women, and what with art? Perhaps women are to him more like works of art than warm human beings; or perhaps he idealises them and his own feeling toward them? What manner of man is it that seeks 'the secret of life'? Is he one of those people, not infrequent amongst analysts as well as patients, who cherish the idea that there is some one system of thought which will provide a complete explanation of life and answers to all its problems. If this is so, is the dream revealing another, more sceptical aspect of the dreamer's personality which is accepting that the secret of life cannot be wholly grasped or comprehended? Perhaps his whole life has been a futile striving after the impossible, and the dream reflects his despair.

It might very well have turned out to be appropriate to go into all these matters during the course of this patient's therapy, even if he had not had this dream. But the dream raises these questions direct. Because it is a spontaneous product of the patient's own mind which he has not willed, it leads straight into problems which might not have come to the surface for many weeks. This is an example of a dream which seems to epitomise the dreamer's attitudes and difficulties within a small compass. Although a good deal of research has been carried out, especially since the discovery of REM sleep, we are still far from knowing all there is to know about dreams; so that dogmatic interpretation of them is inappropriate. Like works of art, dreams must often be allowed to speak for themselves. The seventeenth-century physician, Sir Thomas Browne, wrote: 'However dreames may bee fallacious concerning outward events, yet may they bee truly significant at home, & whereby wee may more sensibly understand ourselves. Men act in sleepe with some conformity unto their awaked senses, & consolations or discoureagments may bee drawne from dreames, which intimately tell us ourselves.'[4] Three hundred years later, I doubt if we can improve upon this statement.

Psychotherapists should also take account of day-dreams. These are more easily understood than dreams, since, although largely emotionally determined, consciousness imposes a certain coherence upon them which is lacking in night dreams. Everyone has day-dreams, although it is sometimes hard to get people to reveal them. Indeed, it has been stated that all of us have something like a 'B-movie' going on all the time just below the level of our directed awareness; a movie in which we play the leading part or parts. In Chapter 4, I suggested that many people were preoccupied with a monologue like that attributed by James Joyce to Molly Bloom at the end of *Ulysses*. Nearly everyone seems to have day-dreams of success and also of sexual fulfilment; of what it would be like to be very rich, or Prime Minister, or a great writer or painter, or of how nice it would be to go to bed with the pretty girl opposite one in the 'bus. In *Childhood, Boyhood, Youth*, Tolstoy writes:

'Let me not be reproached if the day-dreams of my adolescence were as puerile as those of my childhood and boyhood. I am convinced that if I am destined to live to extreme old age, and my narrative continues with the years, as an old man of seventy I shall be found dreaming dreams just as impossible and childish as now. I shall be dreaming of some charming Marya who will fall in love with me, a toothless old man, as she fell in love with Mazeppa, and of how my feeble-minded son suddenly becomes a minister of state, or that all of a sudden I shall find myself possessed of millions. I am convinced that there is no human being and no age devoid of this benign comforting capacity to dream.'[5]

However, the fact that they are ubiquitous does not mean that day-dreams are of no interest, or that they cannot shed light upon character.

Day-dreams, like so many mental productions, are Janus-faced. That is, they may be escapist phantasises; a way of avoiding the tasks and difficulties of real life. Or, on the other hand, they may be rehearsals for future actions, or valuable attempts at finding solutions to problems.

Schizoid patients often have day-dreams which are removed from reality, which reflect their isolation and alienation. These day-dreams have much in common with the delusional systems of psychotics, although the schizoid person does not mistake his day-dreams for truth, as does the schizophrenic. Delusional systems, in which the patient phantasies that he is a person of great importance, but which give no hint of any effort on his part which might have led to his achieving eminence, probably begin as day-dreams of an escapist kind which comfort the patient for his failure in life. They then become so essential to his self-esteem that he has to believe in them, and can no longer see them in the light of wish-fulfilling phantasies.

Schizoid patients often become lost in day-dreams, to the detriment of their engagement with the external world. When patients of this kind fail in their studies, or lose the jobs which they are attempting, it is sometimes because the inner world of day-dream has become so seductive that they cannot tear themselves away from it to become involved with mundane tasks. Some such patients have alarming day-dreams which make them feel that their minds are becoming out of control, and that they are threatened by insanity; a fear which is not always unjustified.

The exploration of day-dreams is especially important in cases of people with sexual difficulties. People who have been isolated in childhood and adolescence and who have not shared their experience of developing sexual feelings with contemporaries, tend to develop a sexual life based upon masturbatory day-dreams, often of an extremely unrealistic kind. Since masturbation is a partially rewarding experience, it tends to reinforce the day-dream in such a way that it becomes a fixed pattern which interferes with the patient's capacity to make a sexual relationship with a real person.

There are two entirely opposite kinds of day-dream which

may have this effect. The first, most often encountered in hysterical women, is a day-dream of the kind encountered in women's magazines and the works of 'romantic' novelists. Such tales usually end with the heroine being finally able to secure the affections of a virile, masterful hero who, it is implied, will care for her for ever, making few demands upon her other than that she retain her beauty. The second variety of day-dream, more often encountered in men, is one or other of those sadly stereotyped phantasies which can be found in pornography.

Confession of day-dreams of either kind is often a painful undertaking for patients, but is a necessary precursor to change. It will generally be found that people who are held up at this masturbatory stage of sexual development have a number of other difficulties in forming intimate relationships with people, especially in relating to others physically. The day-dream predominates over a 'real' relationship with another person not only because it itself brings at least some pleasure, but because the alternative, of actual physical intimacy with a separate individual, is either distasteful or frightening or both.

Such are some of the negative aspects of day-dreams. In contrast, many day-dreams are not escapist but, as I wrote above, rehearsals for future actions, or attempts at finding solutions to problems. Some of the greatest achievements of the human mind take origin from day-dreams. The special theory of relativity depended upon Einstein's ability to day-dream about how the universe might appear to be to an observer travelling at the speed of light. Einstein did not attribute his success as a scientist to his superiority in mathematics or physics, but to his imaginative capacity. Other examples of the positive function of day-dreaming can be found in my book on creativity[6] or in Jerome L. Singer's excellent study of the subject.[7]

The psychotherapist will frequently have as patients middle-aged people suffering from depression; especially women whose children have grown up, who feel unwanted; or men who have reached a plateau in their careers and feel they have nothing to aim for. I have found it rewarding to ask such people to recall the day-dreams they had as adolescents. Very often ambitions and interests which were important have had to be discarded during the years in which a family is being raised and a career pursued. Revival of adolescent day-dreams may point the way to a new departure which may once again make life into an exciting exploration instead of a dull routine. The way out of a mid-life crisis may be to develop those sides of one's nature which never had a chance to grow during the years of conventional striving.

When patients find it difficult to describe what they are feeling in words, I sometimes suggest that they should draw or paint their experience. Some will object that they cannot draw; but since it is not works of art for which one is asking this does not matter. Paintings, partly through the use of colour, are often vividly descriptive of a patient's mood, particularly as revealing an underlying depression which may not be manifest in the patient's talk or manner. Paintings are not only useful as revealing the present 'state of affairs', but also have a therapeutic function in themselves. In Chapter 4, I wrote of the distancing effect of putting things into words. Paintings also have this effect; but are often more useful in that they can be kept and looked back upon, whereas words may be forgotten unless recorded. Some patients produce serial paintings which most interestingly record their emotional progress. As in the case of dreams, the novice must not feel that he is obliged to interpret every aspect of a drawing or painting. He may see some things which the patient does not; but it will be the patient who mostly provides his own interpretation. Paintings also provide a useful variety of 'homework' in between psychotherapeutic sessions, which is especially important for patients who are not coming very frequently. The therapist who is treating a patient who is afflicted by moods of rage and despair may be asked: 'But what can I *do* before the next session? Suppose I get into one of my moods?' I have often suggested that the patient should paint it; and a number have found that this enables them to master the mood, rather than continuing to feel at its mercy.

In similar fashion, some patients keep diaries recording both their progress (or lack of progress) in psychotherapy; or simply a detailed record of their own thoughts, moods, and feelings. This can be helpful in exactly the same way as painting. However, whereas very few patients overwhelm the therapist with too many paintings, a number of patients will try to overwhelm him with what they have written to the extent to which, if he were to read it all, the time allotted to that patient's case would be doubled or trebled. One way round this is to throw the responsibility upon the patient by saying: 'Well, there obviously won't be time for me to read all that you have written. Will you please tell me what you discovered in the act of writing which you think was most important; or tell me which part of it you feel needs further exploration?'

I once treated a patient who had recurrent psychotic breakdowns of a very dramatic kind. Whilst she was psychotic, she was beyond the reach of psychotherapy, but, in between episodes was co-operative and anxious for help. Most of the doctors she had seen had encouraged her to ignore the content of her psychosis, and to forget all about her periods of madness once they were over. I took the risk of encouraging her to write an account of her illnesses, taking the view that by this means, she might feel less at the mercy of the illness should it recur. This she did, using a pseudonym, and the book was published.[8] Some fourteen years later during which she had been free of attacks, she wrote to me about another matter, and I enquired whether she felt that writing the book had had any effect upon her health. She has given me permission to quote her reply. 'Yes, it was very good for me to have written the book, and to have done so while the events were vividly in mind. Having done so I'd "got it in the bag" so to speak, and could afford to forget all about it for some years – which was also good for me . . . . If I hadn't written the book, I might have been frightened to get married. But as A. had read it, and was *still* prepared to take the risk of getting married to me, I reckoned it was OK to go ahead.'

I am sure that her marriage after her series of illnesses was more important than her writing in maintaining her stability; but I am also sure that one cannot afford to 'forget all about' very disturbing things in one's own psyche unless one has faced them. Writing about such things is one way of accomplishing this.

References

1.   Freud, Sigmund (1901) *On Dreams*, p. 682. Standard Edition, Collected Works, Vol. 5. London: Hogarth Press (1953).

2. Jung, C. G. (1931) *The Practical Use of Dream Analysis*, p. 147 in *The Practice of Psychotherapy*, Collected Works, Vol. 16. London: Routledge and Kegan Paul (1954).

3. Storr, Anthony (1973) *Jung*. London: Fontana Modern Masters.

4. Browne, Sir Thomas (1977) *On Dreams* in *Sir Thomas Browne: The Major Works*. Harmondsworth: Penguin, p. 477.

5. Tolstoy, Leo (1964) *Childhood, Boyhood, Youth*, p. 184. Harmondsworth: Penguin.

6. Storr, Anthony (1972) *The Dynamics of Creation*. London: Secker and Warburg.

7. Singer, Jerome L. (1974) *Daydreaming and Fantasy*. London: Allen and Unwin.

8. Coate, Morag (1964) *Beyond all Reason*. London: Constable.

7

Objectivity and Intimate Knowledge

In the course of his daily work, the psychotherapist comes to know a considerable number of people extremely intimately. This is surely one of the most rewarding and interesting aspects of the job. Those who practise psychotherapy as a more or less full-time occupation come to know more people more intimately than do members of any other profession. Moreover, psychotherapists know their patients far better than they know their own friends or colleagues, and often better than they know their own spouses or children. Although sexual intimacy appears to many people to be the closest kind of human intimacy, I do not think this is the case. Whilst sexual intimacy often encourages other kinds of intimacy – hence, the war-time convention of the 'beautiful spy' who is used to extract secrets from the enemy officer – a sexual relation may not only render verbal relations less necessary, but also create an illusion of mutual understanding which shatters when the sexual partnership comes to an end. The practice of psychotherapy has made me aware that many husbands and wives know rather little about one another, even when their sexual relationship is satisfactory. Although the psychotherapist is debarred from certain areas of knowledge about his patient because he neither lives with him nor sleeps with him, he is, if he is at all skilled at his profession, likely to acquire more intimate knowledge of his patient than anyone else ever has or will. This is largely a consequence of the time which the therapist gives to each individual he treats; a span unlikely to be matched in any other kind of relationship: and also to the fact that the intimacy is necessarily one-sided. During the time of the therapy, the therapist puts himself at the patient's disposal and refrains from talking about himself. This feature of psychotherapy is difficult to match outside the confessional. The psychotherapist's purpose is to increase the patient's self-knowledge, both by acting as a reflecting mirror in which the patient may descry himself and also by gradually building up a coherent picture of the· patient's personality by making the interpretative connections discussed in Chapter 5. Such a picture can only be drawn after prolonged enquiry. This chapter is designed to explore some of the factors which may interfere with the psychotherapist coming to know his patient as intimately as he needs to do, and also to delineate the kind of attitude toward patients, emotional as well as intellectual, which, to my mind, the psychotherapist should seek to cultivate. In what follows, I assume that the psychotherapist possesses enough intelligence to see connections and make reasonable interpretations; that he is a reliable, consistent person who aims at professional standards; and that he has a genuine interest in human problems and therefore some capacity for empathy.

The first difficulty which the therapist may encounter is to rid himself of his own prejudices. However objective we may think we are or attempt to be, we never approach a new person as if he was entirely an unknown quantity. More especially, if we are interested in a new person, as the therapist is, or hopes to be, in his patient, we begin trying to 'place' him. Suppose, for example, that you are travelling by train and find yourself attracted (or repelled) by the face of a stranger opposite. 'He looks like a business man', you say to yourself: and, depending upon your imaginative capacity and the degree of your interest, you may carry your speculation further, to include the man's age, family, dwelling place, type of business, and so on. Nature abhors a vacuum; and we fill the Rorschach silhouettes of personality with which unknown persons present us from our own experience; the store of memories derived from our previous encounters with which all our minds are, inevitably, furnished. In origin, this 'placing' activity is biologically adaptive; a kind of safety precaution. Primitive man, encountering a total stranger, needed to know whether he was a friend or foe, and wanted all the clues he could obtain in order to know how to approach and address the unknown person.

However, our experience of people in the past cuts both ways. Without it, we should not know how to approach new people at all: with it, we are liable to misconceptions which have to be corrected and discounted if we are to know the person as he really is. Thus, if we have been brought up to believe that all red-haired men are short-tempered, we may make the wholly unjustified assumption that the unknown red-haired patient who has just sat down in front of us is short-tempered also. If the patient has an upper-class English accent, we may assume, quite wrongly, that he is arrogant or snobbish. The young or inexperienced therapist often makes assumptions about patients which are derived from his own background, especially in regard to methods of child-rearing and the relations of children with parents. One of the fascinating results of the practice of psychotherapy is that the therapist comes to know a good deal about the differences between people from different social backgrounds. He learns that children in Ilford are reared differently from children in Chelsea: that in some suburban areas, there is intense social competition between households, expressed in material terms; whereas in others, such competition is despised. In England, social class still governs social life in a way which we have not yet learned to overcome, with the result that, whatever part of society we ourselves may come from, we have rather little idea how any other part lives. Beginners in psychotherapy may find themselves overawed by patients who come from a 'superior' social background, or ignorant about those who come from any quite different from their own. However, if the therapist is content to remain a passive listener in the way described in Chapter 3, he will find that the patient will usually give him enough information for him to avoid making tactless mistakes. As an example of such a mistake, I recall the case of a man who was seeking analytical treatment from a Continental analyst of wide experience. He happened to belong to an ancient family, and to have been brought up on a large country estate (long since made over to the National

Trust). As she listened to his account of his adolescent development, the analyst was unable to understand his lack of early sexual experience. 'But surely', she said, 'you must have had the peasant girls on your father's estate?' Lack of appreciation of the kind of upbringing an English schoolboy in his situation was likely to have had, together with incomprehension of the relation between English landowners and their tenants could hardly be more complete. However, even greater cultural differences can be overcome provided the therapist is prepared to listen and learn rather than jump in with premature comments. A Ghanaian therapist trained in this country has convinced me that even the immense differences between his own experience of family life and that of any patient he is likely to encounter in England are not unbridgeable. However, it took him many months to educate his training analyst to understand his own background.

Beginners may also be ill-at-ease when confronted with patients who are older, more intelligent, and more gifted than they are themselves. It is helpful to remember that even the most impressive persons started life as helpless infants; that very high intelligence may march hand-in-hand with emotional obtuseness; and more especially, that the psychotherapeutic situation offers a unique opportunity for self-exploration which the patient, however sophisticated, will never have encountered before unless he has had previous psychotherapy. Provided that his initial technique of facilitating a free flow of talk on the part of the patient is adequate, the beginner will find that most patients will disregard his inexperience, even if they had ever been aware of it. I was once involved in the supervision of a doctor who had embarked upon the psychotherapeutic treatment of her very first patient. As he was an exceptionally highly educated man who was older than she was, more experienced, better read, and probably more intelligent, she was somewhat overawed. However, when he came to see me to report progress, he commented that his therapist was obviously well trained! As he gets to know his patient, the therapist will find that his sense of awe diminishes, since it is one of those projections deriving from the therapist's own childhood, when 'grown-ups' seemed inaccessibly high above him.

Disappearance of awe does not, of course, involve any

diminution of respect, or any loss of appreciation of the ways in which patients may be one's intellectual, social, and moral superiors. Indeed, the more one gets to know other people intimately, the more one respects the ways in which human beings manage to retain courage and dignity in the face of what may be grave emotional hazards.

Apart from difficulties of the kind already outlined, the therapist may find himself confronted by other prejudices of his own. Some therapists (Jung was one; Reich another) are prejudiced against homosexuals. Women therapists find dependence and passivity in male patients hard to tolerate. Male therapists are often put off by dominance and assertiveness in women. In such cases, the therapist does well to take a closer look at himself. Most of the traits we most deplore in others have their place within the recesses of our own psyches; and it is perhaps this fact which most demands that the doctor who wishes to practise psychotherapy as his major professional activity should himself be the subject of analysis.

Perhaps the commonest difficulty which therapists in training encounter is that of remaining relatively passive. In Chapter 3 I said that doctors who are not used to practising psychotherapy find it difficult to abandon their traditionally authoritarian role. The conventional medical consultation nearly always ends with the doctor giving the patient some instructions, even if these be no more than details about the further investigations which are needed. Doctors, particularly, feel ill-at-ease if they are not handing out something to the patient; a regime, a prescription, or advice: and the more inexperienced they are, the more they feel the need of doing something other than just listening. In a later chapter, I shall discuss a number of aspects of the personality of people who are particularly attracted to the practice of psychotherapy. Such people, on the whole, are not executives by nature. They do not like issuing orders, arranging the lives of others, making decisions, constructing plans. Psychotherapists do not make good administrators and generally try to leave administration to others. This tendency toward passivity is an advantage in the practice of psychotherapy, but is not a trait necessarily found in doctors who are learning about psychotherapy only as part of their training. Doctors tend often to be active rather than contemplative; practical people who enjoy manipulating gadgets, using apparatus, changing the external world. They are – to use Liam Hudson's classification – convergers rather than divergers; scientists rather than artists, albeit with many exceptions. Such people find it hard to tolerate the passivity required of the psychotherapist, whose function is that of a mid-wife rather than that of a surgeon. Some of those who are directive by nature can learn to hold their tendency to issue orders in check; others cannot. The latter are unlikely to become good psychotherapists.

Those in training often ask whether it is necessary for them to like their patients if they are to help them. This question generally arises during preliminary interviews, more especially when the doctor has a particular prejudice of the kind mentioned earlier in this chapter. If, on serious examination of his own negative preconceptions and their origins, a doctor continues actively to dislike a patient who has been referred to him, it may be better for him to cease working with that particular patient; but this problem very rarely arises in actual practice. I have seen a number of patients to whom I did not instinctively take at first; but if we have been able to continue working together, I have almost always come round to liking them. Coming to know another person very intimately and active dislike are generally incompatible; and the only patients I have continued to find unlikeable are those whom I have not had time or opportunity to get to know well. Another rewarding aspect of the practice of psychotherapy is that one enlarges one's capacity for liking people whom one may not find initially attractive.

Psychotherapists are far more likely to encounter difficulties because they like their patients too much rather than because they like them too little. One danger is too close an identification with the patient. That is, a psychotherapist may be so intensely sympathetic with the patient's difficulties, and so entirely capable of putting himself in the patient's shoes, that he loses the objectivity required to see in what way the patient is failing to deal with his problems. Many years ago I took over the treatment of an intelligent woman from a distinguished woman psychiatrist who had been seeing her for some time. For a long time, I could not make out what had been going on in these previous sessions. Finally, I asked her to tell me more about them. 'Oh', she said: 'We just sat and chatted about how dreadful men were.' It was obvious that the therapist had found so much in common with the patient that all objectivity had been lost, and the sessions had deteriorated into a mutually sympathetic exchange in which all possibility of dynamic progress had disappeared. Since both doctor and patient may enjoy such exchanges, sessions of this kind may go on for some time without either party complaining or even realising that 'nothing is happening'.

A passionate desire to help people with whose problems the therapist feels a particular sympathy may sometimes have undesirable consequences. One psychiatrist found himself unable to bear the tears of his women patients, and hastened to comfort them by putting his arms round them. This practice sometimes led to his becoming sexually involved with them; not because he was deliberately exploiting them, but because his intense desire to relieve their misery led to his offering love as a direct way of bringing comfort. Today, when 'encounter groups' in which physical contact between participants is encouraged as breaking down barriers, therapists in training sometimes ask whether the analytical rule that the therapist should not have physical contact with his patients ought always to be strictly observed. The example given shows how easy it is to deceive oneself. By entering into physical relations with his patients, the psychiatrist was obstructing their progress toward finding ways of fulfilling their own needs independently. He was also, implicitly, promising more than he could perform since, as a result of his actions, his patients would be bound to entertain phantasies of marriage, or at least of an exclusive, 'special' relationship, and to be angry and disappointed when their hopes were not realised. Moreover, the psychiatrist, apart from running the risk consequent upon infringing the code of medical ethics, was gaining sexual gratification for himself without taking the risk of being rejected or facing any of the other hazards and responsibilities which normally accompany sexual involvement between peers in ordinary life. He was a diffident man who had always been uncertain of himself when approaching the opposite sex. The therapeutic situation offered him a 'safe' way of gaining the love of women; a fact of which he was insufficiently aware.

A less obvious way in which therapists can exploit their patients is by unwittingly encouraging their dependence. Even the most self-deprecating psychotherapist is bound to acknowledge that he obtains gratification from having a number of patients who turn to him, look up to him, and value him as perhaps the only human being in whom they have felt able fully to confide. We all want to be valued by other human beings, and psychotherapists are no exception. Psychotherapists in full-time practice are apt to collect a number of 'good' patients who come regularly, who are grateful for what the therapist has to offer them, who produce interesting dreams or other 'material', and who, if the therapist is in private practice, pay their bills regularly. Because of the good relationship obtaining between them, the patient is apt to overlook the fact that therapy cannot be a substitute for life; whilst the therapist may be unaware that the patient's dependency on him is providing him with a boost to his own self-esteem. The danger in such a situation is that the patient's progress toward autonomy is brought to a halt, whilst the treatment goes on indefinitely. Only if the therapist is fully aware of this danger will he be constantly vigilant to interpret the patient's dependence, to point out in what way he is relying upon the therapist rather than upon himself, and to encourage him to do without therapy rather than persist in it. Within the National Health Service, it is seldom possible to offer patients psychotherapy which is prolonged to the extent I have just described, but such cases do occasionally happen. Even the most experienced psychotherapist ought, I suggest, to discuss with a colleague those cases in which the patient appears to be making good progress but in which no obvious end to the treatment ever appears to come into view. Psychotherapists are often criticised by those who do not know much about psychotherapy for the length of their treatments, and these criticisms are sometimes justified. However, there are a small number of cases in which psychotherapy needs to be extremely prolonged, and even cases which last ten or more years are not necessarily instances of misjudgement or exploitation. No-one reading Marion Milner's[1] account of a psychoanalytic treatment lasting more than twenty years, *The*

Hands of the Living God, could possibly think that the patient was exploited, although they might think that the analyst herself was setting impossibly high standards of professional devotion.

I wrote earlier that the therapist was far more likely to get into difficulties because he liked his patients too much rather than because he liked them too little.

The patients with whom the therapist is likely to feel the most intense sympathy are generally those whose psychopathology in some way resembles his own. Thus, the therapist who has himself been lonely will feel particular compassion for the isolated; or one who has been ill-at-ease with his own physical being will find it easier to understand the way in which schizoid patients become alienated from the body. Sympathy of this kind is likely to lead to the inexperienced therapist telling the patient about some of his own difficulties, past or present, in exactly the same way as he might say to a friend in distress; 'I know how you feel; I've been through it myself.'

Although the psychotherapist gets to know his patient very intimately, the patient does not, and should not, get to know the therapist in the same way. Doctors beginning psychotherapy often share the patient's conviction that this is unfair. They feel that it might be helpful to the patient if they revealed their own problems, since it would convince him that they understood what it is to be depressed or anxious from the inside. Or they feel that it is somehow pretentious not to reveal oneself; setting oneself up as superior; pretending to a state of maturity or balance which one has not, in fact, attained. However, there are a number of good reasons why it is important that the therapist does not yield to the temptation of revealing himself to the patient. The first is that, if he does so, he will deprive himself of a valuable source of information about the patient. For, just as we have seen that the therapist is bound to have phantasies about the patient, so, equally, the patient is bound to have phantasies about the therapist. In any psychotherapeutic treatment which is at all deep or prolonged, exploration of the phantasies which the patient has about the therapist will be an important part of the treatment. If the patient knows too much about the therapist he will not have so many phantasies about him. Although the therapist cannot, of course, be an entirely 'blank screen', since he is bound to reveal a good deal about himself by his manner of speech, his dress and appearance, and other pointers, he will find out more about the patient if he refuses to answer questions about his personal life than if he does not. For example, many patients will want to know whether or not the therapist is married. Rather than answer such a question direct, it is important to throw the question back, by enquiring what difference the patient would feel if the therapist was married, on the one hand, or was not on the other. Suppose the patient is a male homosexual and the therapist is also male. The patient may be hoping that the therapist is unmarried because he feels that only another homosexual will be able to understand what he feels. If he knows that the therapist is married, the patient may not only make the damaging assumption that there are areas of his experience which the therapist will not be able to comprehend, but will fail to discuss the difficulties he has in relationships with heterosexuals.

Suppose the patient is a woman, and the therapist is a male. Her anxiety to know whether or not the therapist is married may be because she has a phantasy of being married to him herself; a phantasy which might never become explicit if she knew that the therapist was married. Exploration of such a phantasy may lead on to all kinds of discoveries about the patient's wishes and fears in regard to men which would greatly aid her understanding of herself and her difficulties in relationships.

Second, it is inadvisable to tell patients of one's own psychological difficulties and problems in the way one might share one's own experiences with a friend who is in trouble because, in the therapeutic relationship, one is not a friend but a therapist. Of course one is drawing on one's own experience of life when trying to understand another person's feelings; but it is not therapeutic to say: 'Yes, I know what it is like to be depressed, I've been terribly depressed too', even if this is true. Patients of course realise that therapists have their problems, and the more sophisticated know that it is not by accident that the therapist became interested in psychotherapy; but, whilst they are in treatment, what they want and need is a therapist whom they can trust, and upon whom they can rely, not some one whom they perceive as wrestling with unsolved problems of his own. This is especially true in the early stages of therapy. When patients begin treatment, they are often extremely anxious and unsure both of themselves and of the therapist. It is only when they become more confident themselves that they can afford to see the therapist as the fallible human being which, like other human beings, he is bound to be.

When I was young and inexperienced, a man once came to see me whose principal problem was intense guilt about masturbation. His sessions with me were progressing fairly well, when one day he suddenly asked me, just as he was about to leave the room, whether I had ever masturbated. Without thinking, caught off my guard, I answered 'Yes'. I never saw that patient again. What I ought to have said was something like this. 'What reply are you hoping for? Are you wanting me to say "No" because someone who has never masturbated is a kind of ideal to you?' and then explored his phantasy further. It would probably have emerged that he had never been able to imagine his parents as sexual beings, and that he had completely unrealistic notions about male sexuality in general; but my thoughtless admission clearly disillusioned him about me to such an extent that he felt I could be of no use to him. Although it is quite understandable that therapists do not want to set themselves up as god-like beings without problems, this example illustrates that revealing things about oneself which one may think of as trivial may be regarded by the patient in quite a different light. There is a sense in which a therapist is, for the time being, assuming the mantle of a secular priest. In going to a priest to confess one's sins, one may know perfectly well that the priest too is a sinner; but one would not want him to be telling one his sins at the time when his role is to absolve one from one's own.

In fact, revealing things about himself is, for the therapist, nearly always a form of self-indulgence, however much he may try to believe that it is for the patient's benefit. Therapists want acceptance and understanding from people just as do their patients; but they should not use a psychotherapeutic session for this purpose. When therapists reveal themselves to their patients, the situation changes from therapy into a mutual exchange; an ordinary relationship of the kind which obtains between friends, and therefore one in which the therapist is obtaining the kind of gratification which occurs in mutual exchanges between friends. The therapist's job is to understand his patient, not to obtain understanding from his patient. Whilst he is acting as therapist, he is the patient's agent. He is there simply to serve the patient; and, although he may legitimately enjoy the gratification of using his special skills, of earning a living and of feeling that he is doing a good job, he should not be seeking any other form of reward.

Psychotherapy is bound to be a one-sided relationship for the reasons I have just given. Patients often complain about this, especially in the later stages of therapy, and may accuse the therapist of trying to keep them in an inferior position by refusing to reveal any details of his own life. One can indicate that one is sympathetic to this wish without yielding to it. Analysis of the patient's desire for the therapist to disclose more of himself often brings to light the patient's habitual feeling of inferiority to others, combined with his wish to denigrate or topple from their perch those whom he feels to be superior. The therapist will want to explore such feelings and may, at the same time, point out that such exploration would not be possible if the therapist were to start talking about himself. Although psychotherapists need to draw upon all the understanding of their own personalities that they possess, as well as upon their experience of others, their task is not to affirm or express their own personalities whilst practising psychotherapy, but to act as a mirror in which the patient can ever more clearly discern his own. As we shall see in a later chapter, this self-abnegatory posture has its effect upon the therapist himself; and he may feel the need to compensate for his lack of self-expression in his professional life by finding other ways in which he can affirm himself outside his practice. Some therapists, after a very few sessions, call their patients by their Christian names. I have usually avoided this practice. If I call the patient by his Christian name whilst he continues to call me 'Dr Storr' the patient's position as 'child' is underlined, and this is denigrating. If we both use Christian names, the relationship may seem less professional and more like ordinary friendship.

What I have just written might lead some people to suppose that I am advocating the kind of remote, detached, impersonal attitude which convention associates with psychoanalysts. Nothing could be further from the truth. Research has shown that patients do better if they perceive the therapist as warm and sympathetic; and they are more likely to perceive him in this way if he is genuinely warm and sympathetic and not afraid to show his feelings in his tone of voice. If the therapist tries to protect himself from entering into his patient's feelings by being detached, he will cut himself off from an important avenue of understanding what the patient is feeling, and will be less effective as a therapist. Psychotherapy is, and, in my view, should be, emotionally demanding of the therapist; and if, at the end of his day's work, he does not feel somewhat drained, I doubt if he will have accomplished much therapeutically. However, he must retain enough objectivity to see in what way the patient is failing to cope with his problems and contributing to them. Empathy without objectivity is as little use as objectivity without empathy. The therapist has to walk a tight-rope between over and under-identification with his patient. If he so over-identifies with him as to lose his power to criticise, he will not be able to see how the patient should change. If he remains as critically detached as if he was performing a scientific experiment, he will not be able to understand his patient as a person or appreciate the difficulties which he faces. It is because of this that the practice of psychotherapy will always remain more of an art than a science.

Jung once wrote: 'If the doctor wants to guide another, or even accompany him a step of the way, he must *feel* with that person's psyche. He never feels it when he passes judgement. Whether he puts his judgements into words, or keeps them to himself, makes not the slightest difference. To take the opposite position, and to agree with the patient offhand, is also of no use, but estranges him as much as condemnation. Feeling comes only through unprejudiced objectivity. This sounds almost like a scientific precept, and it could be confused with a purely intellectual, abstract attitude of mind. But what I mean is something quite different. It is a human quality — a kind of deep respect for the facts, for the man who suffers from them, and for the riddle of such a man's life.'[2]

Jung's 'unprejudiced objectivity', is, therefore, underpinned with a respect for the human being which is neither unprejudiced nor wholly objective. He is on the patient's side, however much he deplores some of the things the patient does, or disagrees with his opinions. Carl Rogers refers to 'unconditional positive regard' as being the attitude on the part of the therapist which is most helpful to the patient. Because coming to know another human being very intimately almost always involves coming to like that human being, there is a sense in which psychotherapists are bound to lose some discrimination in regard to their patients. Just as one is inclined to excuse conduct in members of one's own family which one might condemn in others, so one is inclined to be indulgent towards the faults of one's patients. There is a sense in which a psychotherapist's geese all tend to turn into swans. I think this inevitable, and, from the patient's point of view, not wholly undesirable. For one of the factors which helps in psychotherapy is undoubtedly the conviction that there is at any rate one person who is entirely 'on one's side'; who is, for the time that one is with him, wholly dedicated to one's interests.

A good deal of this chapter has been concerned with discussing what is often referred to as 'counter-transference'; that is, in the wider sense of the term, the therapist's emotional attitude toward his patient. Part of counter-transference seems to me to be an irrational prejudice in favour of those whom, as a therapist, one comes to know intimately. This sometimes means that critics accuse psychotherapists of spending too much time trying to treat people whom they themselves rate lowly. Psychotherapy is a scarce resource, and the critics may sometimes be right. It remains true that an irrational prejudice in favour of the damaged, the despised, the insulted and injured, is better than an irrational prejudice against them. It is, in my view, a therapeutic factor of considerable importance.

References
1. Milner, Marion (1969) *The Hands of the Living God*. London: Hogarth Press and Institute of Psycho-Analysis.
2. Jung, C. G. (1932) *Psychotherapists or the Clergy* in *Psychology and Religion*. Collected Works, Vol. 11, pp. 338–9. London: Routledge and Kegan Paul (1958).

8

Transference

In the last chapter, I said that getting to know another person partly consisted of the correction of misconceptions, since we all 'project' upon an unknown person images derived from our experience of others in the past. I also said that the phantasies which the patient has about the therapist were an important source of information. If, for example, the patient approaches every new person he meets with the phantasied expectation that that person will despise him or be critical of him, his capacity for making friends will be greatly impaired. Another way of looking at this phenomenon is to see it as an example of conditioning. If a person's early childhood has been one in which he was illtreated and rejected, it is likely that he will have been conditioned to expect such treatment from any new person whom he encounters. We do not approach new people as if they were blank sheets, but 'transfer' what we have already experienced from the past into the present.

This process, which is an inevitable part of ordinary life, takes on a special form in the psychotherapeutic situation, for two reasons. The first is the maintenance by the therapist of comparative anonymity. His refusal to correct the patient's misconceptions by revealing personal details about himself allows the exploration and discussion of those misconceptions in a way which would not be possible if they were to be immediately corrected. The second is that, since the patient is asking for help, he is, automatically and inescapably, in the position of regarding the therapist as an authority. Directly we treat another human being as an authority, we are particularly apt to endow that person with some of the attributes of the authorities whom we have encountered in the past; and, for most people, the most significant authorities from the past are, of course, their parents.

The tendency to project upon the therapist attributes belonging to the patient's parents will be reinforced by the fact that, in any psychotherapeutic treatment which is at all prolonged, revival and reliving of the emotions connected with the patient's childhood is inescapable. Although psychotherapists today do not lay as much emphasis as did Freud upon the recovery of buried memories or the recall of forgotten traumata, most would agree that the patient's early years are important in shaping his adult character, and that the emotional climate of those early years significantly determined his attitudes to other people and to the various challenges with which life confronts all human beings.

It is also the case that, whenever we 'look after' another person, we are to some extent taking on the role of a caring, nurturing parent. Although one of the main objectives of psychotherapy is to enable the patient more effectively to care for himself, and thus obviate the need for parent figures by becoming his own parent, the emotional situation which prevails in the early stages of therapy, when the therapist is faced with a person who may be acutely distressed, is bound to be analogous to a parent-child relationship. For have not all of us, unless particularly deprived, had the experience of being comforted by a parent when hurt or disappointed? And is it not the case that, although the therapist may not offer comfort direct, the fact that he is prepared to listen and to try to understand puts him automatically into a 'parental' category?

When Freud first encountered and described the phenomenon of transference, he regarded it as an obstacle to therapy. It also seems probable that Freud did not wish to become emotionally important to his patients, but would have preferred to be regarded in the same light as, say, a surgeon; that is, as a technical expert whose field of expertise happened to be the mind rather than the body. However, by 1907, when Jung first visited Freud in Vienna, his views had changed.[1] He asked

Jung what he thought of transference; and when Jung replied
'It is the alpha and omega in treatment', Freud said; 'You have
understood.'

My own belief is that Jung and Freud were right. Transference, (and I am now using the term in its widest sense, that is, as
comprising the whole gamut of the changing relationship
between the patient and the therapist) is the most important
single factor in therapy. Here again, the psychotherapeutic
situation is unique. For what the therapist tries to do is to
understand and interpret the patient's attitude to him, and by
this means to help the patient understand his difficulties in
relationship with others. Let me give an example. I was asked to
see a girl of twenty-two who had made a suicidal attempt, and to
assess whether or not she was suitable for psychotherapy. She
was fluent verbally, and was telling me about some of her
difficulties in relationship with other people when she suddenly
broke off. 'Can't you say something?' she asked. 'I'm doing all
the talking, and you are just sitting there listening. I can't bear
your silence.'

I said something to the effect that, as she was talking freely,
there was no need for me to interrupt her, and then went on. 'I
wonder what you were reading into the silence?'

'If you don't talk, I don't know what you are thinking of
me.'

'What do you imagine that I might be thinking?'

'I think you might be finding me boring, or that you are
criticising me.'

'It sounds to me as if you always approach people with
negative assumptions; as if you never expect people to find you
interesting or likeable.'

She agreed that this was indeed the case. This particular girl
had lost her mother when she was very young, and had never
managed to get on with her father. She had not had enough love
in early childhood to acquire any sense of being lovable or even
likeable. We went on to discuss how, if one does not like
oneself, one is apt to make the assumption that no-one else will
like one either, and thus approach other people with suspicion
and hostility.

In such a case, the patient's developing, changing relationship with the therapist will be the crucial factor in helping her.

What one hopes will happen is that, over a prolonged period, the patient will gradually come to realise that there is one person in the world who is concerned about her and who is trying to understand her as she is. In favourable cases, this will result in the patient coming to realise that people other than the therapist may also be concerned about her and like her. Just as negative attitudes derived from the past will, at first, colour the patient's attitude to the therapist, so positive attitudes achieved during the process of therapy will be, in most instances, transferred to people outside the consulting room. It is obvious that attitudes to parents and other important figures in a child's early development will tend to be transferred to other people as the child grows up. If a child has experienced nothing but love and kindness at home he will be inclined to expect that strangers will treat him in a similar fashion. If he has been starved of affection or maltreated, he will approach new people with an ingrained expectation of rejection. Psychotherapists deal predominantly, and most successfully, with people who have negative expectations; who believe that nobody wants them, or that nobody can understand them; or who are isolated because they have come to believe that intimacy with another person is a threat. If therapy goes well, the patient will come to feel that there is at least one person in the world of whom this is not true. Just as children generalise from their experience of parents, expecting that others will treat them in the same way as their parents have treated them at home, so patients who have come to regard the therapist as understanding and helpful will, one hopes, generalise from their experience with the therapist, and come to regard the people they meet as at least potentially friendly. Psychotherapy thus becomes what has been called a 'corrective emotional experience', in which negative assumptions about other people are gradually modified by means of the repeated analysis of the patient's changing relationship with the therapist.

It is natural, therefore, that, during the course of therapy, the therapist should, for a time, become emotionally important to the patient. If, for most of one's life, one has felt misunderstood or unappreciated, and then encounters someone who appears to understand and accept one, it is scarcely surprising that this should happen. This emotional valuation of the therapist by the patient is generally known as 'positive transference' as opposed to 'negative transference' which consists of the assumptions of rejection and hostility which have been briefly mentioned above. If therapy is going to be effective at all, negative transference has to be 'resolved': that is, dispelled by the therapist continually detecting the patient's negative attitudes, drawing attention to them, and trying to trace their origin from the patient's experience in the past of rejection and hostility. I gave a brief example above of the kind of way in which a therapist might proceed with a patient who was fearful of being boring and of being criticised. In cases where negative transference cannot be resolved, therapy will come to an end because the patient will break it off. (The same may be true in the less common reverse case, in which the therapist has a 'negative counter-transference' toward the patient which cannot be resolved.) Whereas analysis of negative transference is essential if therapy is to proceed, it might be argued that analysis of positive transference is unnecessary, or indeed inimical to progress. Is it not positively helpful to the patient to regard the therapist in the light of an ever-loving, all-understanding parent who will heal the wounds of the past, and make up for all the incidents of rejection, misunderstanding, pain and loss which have finally forced the patient to seek for help?

The answer is both 'Yes' and 'No'. It is certainly essential to the patient's progress that he regard the therapist in a positive light. But transference projections, because of their origin in childhood experience, are, as Freud recognised, apt to be unrealistic and exaggerated. The more deeply disturbed the patient, and the more he or she is cut off from affectionate relations with others, the more likely is it that the therapist will be exalted to the position of being 'the only person who understands'. In the early stages of such an intense transference, it is wise not to hasten to make interpretations designed to hasten the process of the patient's coming to see the therapist in a more realistic light – not that this would, in any case, always be possible. Although the therapist can never replace the patient's parents, nor entirely make up for whatever may have been missing or thought to be missing in the patient's early childhood, the patient's experience of the therapist as an idealised parent may have a healing effect which premature interpretation would dispel. A sensitive, self-deprecatory therapist may well deplore being regarded, even temporarily, by the patient as an omnipotent worker of miracles, a faultless parent, when he knows himself to be no more than a fallible human being with problems of his own. He must realise, however, that, for the purpose of therapy, he is only partly himself. His function is also to act as a peg upon which the patient can hang the images derived from his own past experience and his present needs; and he must be prepared to accept this role for the time being in much the same way that a priest accepts *his* role as the representative of the Deity during the time he is acting as priest, although he knows perfectly well that he may be as great a sinner as his client.

The therapist may also feel that, if the patient appears to improve because he is seeing the therapist in an unrealistically ideal light, this improvement must necessarily be false or insecurely based. This is not the case. Healing of psychological problems is partially, if not wholly, a symbolic process in which words and images play the major role. A great deal of the healing process is metaphorical; an 'as if' process in which the therapist comes to represent both a series of persons from the patient's past, and also a series of possibilities for the future. Real improvement comes about through symbolic interaction.

As therapy progresses, a number of changes take place in the patient's image of the therapist, with the consequence that the therapist comes to be seen as less God-like, more as an ordinary human being. How does this come about? First, if the patient has been through a stage of irrational adoration, he may gain security from this, and thus not need to project that particular image any longer. This may be thought of as analogous to the small child's progress in emotional development; a progress from regarding the parents as omnipotent and omniscient toward seeing them as more or less ordinary human beings, albeit with a special, significant place in the patient's emotional life. Concurrently, in favourable cases, a process goes on by which the therapist, or rather, the patient's experience of the therapist, becomes an integral part of the patient's own psyche. Kleinian analysts would call this process 'introjection of the therapist as a good object'. This too, is a process which we justifiably assume to take place in small children. The small human comes into the world in a state in which he is singularly ill-equipped to fend for himself. The world is large and potentially alarming, whilst he himself is small and helpless. Gaining confidence depends, in the first place, upon being given confidence. However well-equipped the child may be by inheritance, he needs the presence and the care of reliable, trustworthy adults if he is eventually to learn to rely 'on himself'. I put 'on himself' in inverted commas because it seems probable that what the child learns to rely on is something which he has taken into himself from his experience with good parents; something which is 'himself', yet continues to be recognisable as part of himself which, for a time, is not wholly identifiable as 'I' or the ego.

In the same way, a patient in therapy, through his experience of the therapist as a reliable figure, begins to form within himself a reliable figure to whom he can turn in case of difficulty. In the beginning, this figure may be quite clearly an image of the therapist. More than one patient has told me that, when faced with a problem, they have said to themselves; 'What would Dr Storr say?' although they know quite well that what Dr Storr would actually have said is: 'I don't know exactly what you ought to do; let's try and explore the problem further.' I think that, after a while, my image usually disappears as a definable entity, as of course it should do, just as the image of parents as people one turns to disappears as children grow up.

Patients who are going through a phase in which they are very dependent are often apprehensive as to what will happen when the therapy has come to an end. 'What will I do without you?' they ask. I have often thought it right to explain why it is likely that they will be able to manage perfectly well by giving them an explanation of the kind outlined above.

I hope I shall not be thought either blasphemous or arrogant if I compare the process of introjecting parents or therapists with Christ's teaching about the Holy Ghost. It will be recalled that Christ said to his disciples that, when he was gone, God the Father would send the Comforter, the Holy Ghost, who 'shall teach you all things, and bring all things to your remembrance, whatsoever I have said unto you.'[2] In other words, Christ's actual presence would be replaced by an indwelling spiritual presence derived from, or analogous to, Christ himself.

In some patients the process of introjection does not take place satisfactorily. This has two consequences. First, they tend to remain dependent upon the therapist's actual presence, rather than being able to carry him away with them. Second, they seem incapable of transferring their trust in the therapist to other people, so that the therapist tends to remain as seeming to be the only person who understands or cares about them. It seems likely that these two phenomena are really one, in that if the patient cannot make the therapist's image part of his own psyche, he cannot project this image upon other people. We know that small children who are temporarily deprived of the mother often become depressed because they cannot conceive of her return. They are dependent upon her actual presence to be assured of her continuing existence. In the ordinary course of events, the child's ability to tolerate absence gradually increases, but it may be that, in cases where a firm tie with the mother has never been established, the person remains particularly vulnerable to absence and particularly incapable of incorporating within himself whatever other people may have to offer him. Whatever the explanation, every psychotherapist will encounter a few patients in whose eyes he remains the only person whom they feel they have ever trusted, and the only person of whose continuing interest they feel assured. How to deal with the problems raised by such patients will be explored in a later chapter.

The temporary idealisation of the therapist often includes an erotic component, especially when the patient is predominantly heterosexual and the therapist is one of the opposite sex. Recognition of this phenomenon has given rise to the popular superstition that the process of psychotherapy consists principally of 'falling in love with the doctor'. It is, of course, only to be expected that the patient's feelings toward the therapist should include sexual feelings in some instances, and many patients have dreams and phantasies in which the therapist plays the part of a lover. Inexperienced therapists, particularly, are apprehensive about dealing with this phenomenon. How are they to go about it? First, I think it is important to understand that sexual needs and dependent needs are ill-assorted partners. Although human beings, unless schizophrenic, remain dependent in the sense that, however grown-up they become, they continue to need human relationships, this 'mature dependence,' as Fairbairn has named it, is very different from the dependence of childhood. Ideally, the choice of a sexual partner should be made from a position of confidence. Adult sexuality is probably the main force which compels the young human being to leave the nest of home; and unless he has achieved sufficient confidence to do this, he will either fail to find a sexual partner or else choose one on whom he can project a parental image. Emancipation from parents is a prerequisite for a satisfactory love relationship on equal terms; and many marriages which go wrong do so because one partner treats the other like a parent instead of as an equal.

Since the patient endows the therapist with attributes which are predominantly parental, for the reasons given above, it follows that, when erotic elements coincide, the patient is trying to make the therapist into a combination of parent and lover. Freud's explanation of this phenomenon was to postulate that the patient was still erotically tied to the parent of the opposite sex, since he assumed that the erotic tie, rather than the dependent one, was what prevented people from growing up. The child's wish to be united with the parent of opposite sex and eliminate the parent of the same sex is, of course, the notorious Oedipus complex. While not denying that children have sensual wishes and exhibit the precursors of adult sexuality both in behaviour and in phantasy, it has long seemed to me a pity that Freud did not lay more emphasis upon the dependent component of the persistent tie with parental figures which undoubtedly afflicts the majority of neurotics. If dependency rather than a sexual tie is given pride of place in accounting for the need for parental love and understanding which is so evident in patients, it makes more sense to me both of the Oedipus complex and of the incest taboo. If the incest taboo between parent and child is infringed, the child is not only subject to all the dangers which threaten when sexual relations occur between partners of greatly unequal strength and authority, such as being cowed, bullied, frightened and so on, but is also prevented from growing up and leaving home to deal with the external world on his own and become autonomous. If sex is laid on at home together with parental care and support, there is much less reason to grow up and become independent. The wish that the parent or parent substitute should also become a lover can therefore be seen as a way of evading life's tasks and problems; of having the best of both worlds, the world of the child and the world of the adult. Whereas Freud conceived of his patients as being held up in the present by their inability to free themselves from their fixations upon the past, Jung believed that regression to past fixations was often the consequence of difficulties in the present. There is much to be said for Jung's point of view. Take for example, the effects of bereavement. Patients undergoing that particular emotional stress often become like dependent children for a time. So do mothers who have recently been delivered of a new baby. Stress in the present impairs confidence, and makes people revert to patterns of behaviour which, in normal circumstances, they appear to have outgrown.

It is with these conceptions in mind that I approach the problem of erotic manifestations within the transference. It is, of course, out of the question that the therapist should respond to his patient's erotic wishes. This not only infringes the professional code of ethics which governs the relation between patient and therapist, but also prevents the patient from attaining the goal at which the whole of his therapy is aiming, the establishment of true autonomy.

In the practice of his art, the therapist must treat those patients who make declarations of love with tenderness and understanding. It is important to realise that the love which is shown by the patient for the therapist is just as 'genuine', even though it may not be as realistic, as love occurring outside the therapeutic situation. Although the therapist is dealing with aspects of his patient which are predominantly 'childish', he is also dealing with an adult who is as subject as any other to the compulsive need for sexual fulfilment which man's erotic nature imposes upon him.

One manifestation of the patient's feelings toward the therapist which may cause difficulty is the offering of gifts. Gifts from patients may signify a number of different things. Sometimes they are bribes; designed to ensure that the therapist feels under an obligation to the patient and may thus be expected to comply with the patient's wishes in a way which he might not do otherwise. Sometimes gifts are an expression of the patient's wish to establish a 'special', intimate relation with the therapist which is not shared by other patients; or a wish to show, by the nature of the gift chosen, that the patient is especially aware of the therapist's tastes or needs. It is not usually difficult to detect such motives; and this makes refusal of such gifts easy. But sometimes gifts are a genuine manifestation of appreciation, and it is difficult to refuse them without hurting the patient's feelings. In general, it is best to refuse gifts, except at the end of treatment, when a gift may not only signify appreciation on the part of the patient, but may also ease the process of parting. Gifts, at the end of treatment, may be an expression of the fact that the patient feels more on equal terms; that he or she also has 'something to give'. Very occasionally a gift may have to be accepted during treatment if it is something which the patient has created himself. It would be churlish to refuse a book which one's patient had written, or a picture which he had painted; for this is so intimately part of the patient's being that it would be difficult to refuse without causing hurt.

If the therapist has the tact and gentleness to accept love shown to him by his patient without responding to it, but, at the same time, without making the patient feel rejected by him, he will find that, in the course of therapy, the problem usually solves itself. It is possible to interpret these manifestations of erotic love in the way which Freud used, as referring simply to the past; as resuscitations of feelings which belong more properly to the patient's parents. But this is never the whole story, since the erotic feelings which the patient experiences as an adult are different from their precursors which he experienced as a child; and it is, I believe, undervaluing the patient's love to dismiss it as nothing more than a piece of persistent childishness. If the therapist makes it absolutely clear that there is no question, and never can be any question, of responding sexually to the patient, his firmness has the same beneficial effect as the incest taboo; indeed, it is a manifestation of it. That is, it has the effect of making the patient realise that not all his needs can be fulfilled by therapy; that what therapy does is to provide a new base of confidence from which he may go forth better equipped to seek his own fulfilment. It could be said that we all start independent life with a disappointment in love, since the parent of the opposite sex can never be ours. The same is often true of the new start offered by psychotherapy.

In myths and fairy stories, one common theme is the story of the youngest child who is forced by circumstances to leave the shelter of the parental roof to 'seek his fortune'. He usually encounters a great many perils and threats to his life. Often he is required, like Tamino in 'The Magic Flute', to pass a number of tests of courage. Sometimes, as in 'The Sleeping Beauty', or in 'Siegfried', his princess is surrounded by protective barriers of fire or thorn which make her difficult of access. Eventually, the hero overcomes all obstacles, and is rewarded by the hand of the princess. In other words, sexual happiness is the reward for having been brave enough to leave the shelter of the parental home, and face whatever dangers an independent life may confront one with.

The emotions exhibited by the patient toward the therapist may be of any degree of intensity. Although, as I have pointed out, transference is a universal phenomenon, many patients will pass through a period of therapy without showing evidence of profound emotional involvement. However, even in such cases, the therapist should try to make himself aware of the patient's attitudes to himself, and be prepared to investigate these, whenever it seems appropriate. Most, if not all, patients who seek psychotherapy show evidence of disturbance in inter-personal relationships. They will, inevitably, reflect this disturbance in their attitudes to the therapist; and it is when patients become aware of such attitudes in the here-and-now of the therapeutic encounter that they begin to change.

People who approach others with habitual suspicion, for instance; or who are invariably submissive, or who, perhaps, are intellectually arrogant, may be quite unaware (unconscious) that such attitudes interfere with their relations with others. It is only within the therapeutic situation that they are likely to become aware of such things; for it is unlikely that the people they encounter in ordinary life will point these attitudes out without causing offence, and ordinary encounters will not give them the opportunity to change. One reason why psycho-therapy is apt to be a slow business is that changing attitudes takes time and repeated correction. Psychoanalysts refer to this as 'working through'; a phrase which acknowledges the fact that, although certain insights may come in a flash, making use of those insights requires patient application.

References
1. Bennet, E. A. (1961) *C. G. Jung*, p. 34. London: Barrie and Rockcliffe.
2. *The Holy Bible*; Authorised Version. St John XIV, 26.

9

The Hysterical Personality

Before proceeding to discuss some of the difficulties which the psychotherapist may encounter in treating different types of person, I should like to outline what has been said in the previous chapters about the nature of the therapist's task.

His first duty is to provide a secure, reliable background of personal concern against which the patient can develop. Just as a child may be assumed to develop toward maturity in the best way if he is fortunate enough to live in a stable home in which continuing care is taken for granted, so it is assumed that neurotic patients are more likely to learn to understand themselves and to cope better with their personal problems if they are provided with a secure base in the shape of a therapist to whom they can turn as a caring, concerned person.

His second duty is to get to know his patient sufficiently intimately to make sense both of the patient's symptoms and also of his personality as a whole. This involves having a clear picture of how the patient developed from early childhood onwards. Although the acquisition of such understanding does not necessarily abolish all his symptoms nor bring about radical or sudden changes in character structure, it does enable the person to stand back from himself; to look at himself in much the same way as the therapist does, with an eye both critical and sympathetic. The capacity to regard oneself as one, is seems to me to be a prerequisite for change. Neurotic patients who seek psychotherapy do so not because their psychopathology is very different from that of so-called normal people, but because they are overwhelmed or demoralised by their psychopathology. When they can stand back from their own personalities and problems, and apply critical understanding to them, they are on the way to achieving some degree of mastery.

The psychotherapist's third duty is to provide the patient with an opportunity to improve his interpersonal relationships by being a person with whom the patient can interact. He does this first, by providing himself as a more or less unknown quantity upon whom the patient will project the images of those persons who have been emotionally significant to him in the past; and second, by making the patient aware in the here-and-now of how those images and the assumptions which accompany them are interfering with his making positive rela-tionships on equal terms with people he encounters in ordinary life. As the patient's capacity to relate to the therapist without negative assumptions derived from the past increases, so, in most cases, does his capacity to relate to other people outside the therapeutic situation.

I turn now to the consideration of some of the difficulties which the psychotherapist may encounter in applying these principles to the treatment of different types of personality.

The next four chapters are concerned more with types of personality than with discussion of particular neurotic symp-toms. This is because I believe that psychotherapy today is more concerned with understanding patients as whole persons than with the abolition of particular symptoms direct. This topic will be more thoroughly explored in a later chapter. In considering different types of personality, I have adopted the conventional psychiatric classification of hysterical, depressive, obsessional and schizoid. These terms are far from satisfactory, and do scant justice to the extraordinary range and complexity of human character; but they do at least provide a rough categorisation which is better than nothing as a start.

The terms 'hysteria' and 'hysterical personality' are so mis-used as terms of abuse that the heart of the psychotherapist is apt to sink when he hears that a patient with such a label attached is being referred to him. Moreover, he may imagine that he will be unable to understand such a patient, because of his lack of capacity to identify himself with this type of personality. Whilst most psychiatrists are ready enough to admit that they themselves can become depressed, suffer from various forms of anxiety, exhibit some obsessional traits or symptoms, or are capable of the detachment we label schizoid, they are usually very reluctant to recognise or admit the existence of any 'hysterical' components within themselves. Hysterical personalities are therefore apt to seem more alien than the other kinds of people whom the therapist comes across in his work. And yet, hysterical patients were not only those upon whose psychopathology the early structure of psychoanalysis was built, but were also those who seem best to have responded to treatment.

Today the psychotherapist is unlikely to see the dramatic cases of hysteria so vividly described by nineteenth-century psychiatrists. Gross hysterical paralyses, blindness, deafness, 'glove and stocking anaesthesia', fits, tremors and faints have become rare manifestations of neurosis. And, although we may all have patches of amnesia for upsetting happenings which we should rather not recall, fugues, in which the subject experiences massive amnesia for large areas of the past and finds himself in a strange place without knowing how he got there are not phenomena which the psychotherapist practising in outpatient clinics or private consulting-rooms is likely often to encounter. But 'hysterical personalities' who are prone to develop hysterical symptoms of a less dramatic kind are common enough. The best definition of the hysterical personality which I have come across is that given by Slavney and McHeigh (quoted in *The Harvard Guide to Modern Psychiatry*[1]): 'The hysterical personality is dominated by the urgent need to please others in order to master the fear of being unable to do so. This results in restless activity, dramatisation and exaggeration, seductiveness, either social or overtly sexual in manner (often creating disappointment in the other person), and immature and unrealistic dependence upon others.'

The most characteristic feature of an hysterical symptom is that it serves a purpose of which the patient is unaware, or only partially aware. This purpose is, therefore, at first denied by the patient. Hysterical symptoms tend to serve three main purposes. First, they may enable the patient to evade situations which are distasteful, frightening, or potentially humiliating.

'Convenient' headaches are typical hysterical symptoms. Psychotherapists who believe themselves free of hysterical potentialities should search through their memories of childhood. They are likely to find at least one example from their own experience of a physical symptom which conveniently appeared to let them off some boring or alarming occasion, and as conveniently disappeared again when the occasion was safely past.

Second, the symptom may serve the purpose of revenge or punishment of people toward whom the patient feels resentful, whether or not this resentment is objectively justified. Frigidity, for example, is as often a stick with which to beat the patient's husband as it is an expression of distaste for the sexual act.

Third, the symptom may serve the purpose of attracting sympathy or at least attention. Patients of this kind are frightened of making direct demands on people, and therefore draw attention to their distress and need for help by developing symptoms which require that others should pay attention to them.

Patients presenting hysterical symptoms are, therefore, divided selves in that, to the observer, there is an obvious discrepancy between what the patients say they want and feel and what their symptoms make clear that they actually want and feel.

'I wanted to go for a walk, but my legs wouldn't let me.' 'I love my husband, but I can't bear him to touch me.' 'I wanted to die when I took the tablets', but took obvious precautions to ensure that she would be found before there was any chance of dying.

This type of discrepancy arouses in the mind of the doctor the suspicion that the patient is play-acting; a suspicion which may be reinforced when the patient displays emotions of an exaggerated, 'histrionic' kind whether of distress, gratitude, love, or anger. Indeed, to the layman, 'hysterical' and 'histrionic' are almost interchangeable adjectives. In spite of Freud's description of repression, the suspicion remains that the patient is somehow playing false, simulating emotions which she does not feel, denying others which she does feel, and generally making herself out to be someone quite other than she truly is.

It is this characteristic of hysterical patients which doctors find so irritating. It is easy to feel sympathy with the despair of the depressed patient, with the isolation of the schizoid, or with the compulsions of the obsessional. Such patients are obviously 'genuine', however unconscious they may be of their less admirable aspects. But with hysterics, the doubt remains. The discrepancies are too close to the surface to be convincing. If the hysterical patient tries to please, she overdoes it in such a way that the doctor feels that he is being 'manipulated', another pejorative phrase which is constantly applied to such patients. Many hysterical patients try to please by being 'charming'; but the charm is that of an Oriental who is trying to sell one a carpet. One is all the time aware of an ulterior motive.

Doctors rely on the honesty of their patients. Confronted by a patient of whose honesty they feel uncertain, they tend to be nonplussed and then angry, believing that they are being 'pushed around' instead of treated with the respect that, as authorities, they feel they deserve.

Their resentment is understandable, and not wholly unjustified, since it is in practice quite impossible to say how conscious or unconscious a patient may be when conflicting emotions are very near the surface, as in the kind of cases I have been attempting to describe.

At the time of writing, hysterical patients very often come to the notice of psychiatrists by using the device of the 'overdose'. This is an extremely tiresome and dangerous way of drawing attention to one's emotional problems, but a very effective one. Anyone who has attempted to estimate how far any particular patient was genuinely so distressed that she momentarily wished to die, or was primarily making an attack upon her nearest and dearest for neglecting her, or was really hoisting a distress signal, will know that accurate weighing of diverse and complex motives is often impossible.

It is understandable that, in such cases, the doctor should be suspicious and prone to resentment. However, he will never be able to help his patient if he continues to feel such emotions. What he has to do is to control his immediate response sufficiently for him to penetrate a short way beneath the façade presented by the patient. When he is able to do this, he will find a deeply unhappy human being with whom he will be able to sympathise and whom he may be able to help.

Hysterical patients are defeated persons. They do not consider themselves capable of competing with others on equal terms. More especially, they feel themselves to be disregarded, and, as children, often were disregarded in reality. If a child finds that grown-ups do not appreciate his needs or try to meet them when they are made manifest, how does he behave? He becomes demanding, and attention-seeking, exaggerates his needs dramatically, or adopts subterfuges in order to get what he wants indirectly. In trying to understand hysterics, I have found it useful to picture a child who has repeatedly attempted to get his parents to treat him as a person in his own right, but who has repeatedly failed in this endeavour. Many parents pay very little attention to their children's needs, or treat them simply as extensions of their own personalities rather than as individuals with separate identities and requirements.

The deafer parents are, the more the child has to shout to gain their attention. A child who is desperately frightened of going to school, but who knows that, if he were to admit such a fear openly, his parents would dismiss it as 'silly', may shout, scream, or threaten to run away or commit suicide in order to have his feelings taken seriously. Or, if direct appeals prove ineffective, he may find that indirect ones will work. Physical illness is generally accepted as a valid reason for not attending school, and also has the advantage of ensuring at least some additional attention from adults. No wonder that children in desperate straits develop illnesses which serve this double purpose.

Patterns of behaviour of this kind are adopted by children because, at the time, they were the only ones which worked; the only way in which they could persuade adults to pay attention to their needs. When such patterns persist inappropriately into adult life, we label them 'hysterical'. Since hysterics commonly feel unlovable as well as ineffective, they often try to make themselves appear sexually irresistible. Since women are allowed more exhibitionistic licence than men in our culture, these efforts are more obvious in their case. Psychotherapists become accustomed to the phenomenon of the girl who dresses and makes up like a model, but who complains that she is actually frigid. Such girls often learn all the tricks of seduction, but habitually prove disappointing to the males whom they persuade into bed. Some remain as 'cock-teasers', holding out promises which they never in fact fulfil. It is easy to criticise the excessive attention which such girls pay to their appearance as 'narcissistic' (another psychiatric term which has come to be used abusively), and to forget that such attention is a symptom of neglect. It is those who have never received enough attention who lavish attention upon themselves.

The stage as a profession has a particular appeal for hysterics, and some of the most successful actors and actresses belong to this personality type. There are a number of reasons why this should be. First, the stage provides an opportunity for the dramatic display of emotion; something at which hysterical personalities are often expert, since they learned the techniques in childhood. Second, actors and actresses, if at all successful, are approved and applauded by the crowd. This collective adoration is extremely gratifying to someone who has not felt appreciated by his own family and who consequently has no inner conviction of being personally acceptable. To be a public figure is rewarding even though the rewards are superficial and the fidelity of the public less reliable than that of a spouse or parent. Third, actors are, by definition, playing parts; pretending to be someone other than themselves. As we have seen, hysterics, because they have failed to gain what they want by being themselves, are prone to adopt all kinds of masks and roles which they hope will be more acceptable to those around them. In doing so, they tend to lose touch with any sense of continuity in their own personalities; to lose any sense of an inner core which constitutes the 'real I'. People of this type feel that they do not exist as individuals in their own right, and dread being alone because they are then confronted with an inner emptiness. Such individuals, paradoxically, feel more real when they are acting. They only come alive when acting a part.

Successful psychotherapy with patients of this type is almost wholly dependent upon the establishment of a positive transference. Although such patients are sometimes highly intelligent, they are seldom intellectuals. Consequently, insight plays less part in their improvement than does the emotional conviction that, in the therapist, they have found one person who understands and appreciates them.

The establishment of a stable conviction of this kind does not, of course, come overnight; and there are often many ups and downs and tests of the therapist's patience on the way. Because these patients are passionately anxious to find someone who understands and cares for them, and, at the same time have almost lost hope of ever finding such a person, they are apt to behave 'badly' in order to find out whether the therapist will be able to tolerate this. Thus, appointments may be missed without good reason; or, if the therapist is in private practice, accounts may be overlooked and their payment postponed. During the sessions themselves, patients often accuse the therapist of lack of sincerity. 'You don't really care about me, it's just a job to you, a way of making a living.' If the psychotherapist is young and relatively inexperienced, the patient may pick this up and use it as a weapon against him. Any psychotherapist who is a doctor will be listed in the Medical Directory, where the patient may easily find his date of qualification, the degrees he has obtained and what medical posts he has held. If one is young and vulnerable, it is difficult not to react to such a patient's accusations either by angrily refusing to go on treating him, or else by becoming depressed at one's own inadequacy as a therapist. However, if one can hold on to the realisation that the patient's accusations spring from a deep unhappiness, and that unless the patient had some hope that the therapist was not really as black as he was painting him, he would not be coming to ask for his help, it will generally be possible to work through this negative stage.

Some patients alternate between idealisation of the therapist and vicious attacks upon him. I have had patients who, during one session, would extol me as uniquely kind, understanding, perceptive and sympathetic and at the very next would abuse me as useless, cruel, insensitive and altogether hateful. One such patient, terrified that I would dismiss her, would write me deeply apologetic letters after every 'negative' session.

Such patients are profoundly deprived and unhappy people who are generally suffering from the effects of maternal neglect throughout their early childhood. When they do form attachments to people, they repeat over and over again the disappointments of their childhood, because they make impossible demands upon their chosen objects, and then become furiously angry with them when those demands are not met. One woman attached herself to a series of mother-substitutes whom she worshipfully adored during the honeymoon stages of the relationship. As, however, she demanded absolutely exclusive attention, and became intensely jealous if she thought that her beloved paid any attention whatever to anyone else, her relationships always went wrong. Her rage did not confine itself to verbal expression, and she received at least one prison sentence for inflicting 'grievous bodily harm' upon a woman who had taken pity on her. It is unlikely that the inexperienced therapist will have referred to him hysterical patients who 'act out' to this extent. Such people are likely to have attached to them another psychiatric label of a pejorative kind – the term 'psychopath' – and to be adjudged unsuitable for psychotherapy. However, even if his patients are sufficiently controlled to verbalise their emotions rather than act upon them, the emotions are likely to be of much the same kind. What I am trying to convey is that, in dealing with some of the more deeply disturbed hysterics, psychotherapists may find themselves confronted with emotions of an extremely violent and primitive kind which they themselves may find disturbing. Provided that the therapist remains calm in the face of abuse, he will usually find it possible to understand and sympathise with the patient's feelings, and to interpret them in terms of the patient's actual experience in childhood. Thus, if the patient accuses the therapist of neglect or rejection, the therapist might say: 'I'm sure that you have felt rejected in this way by other people before me. In fact, it always seems to happen, doesn't it? Can you remember when you first felt as you are feeling now?' In this way, it is often possible to disclose a long history of repeated patterns of hope followed by disappointment, and to show the patient that it is because her hopes are so exaggerated that they are always doomed to failure.

Or the therapist can attempt to delineate what aspects of his own behaviour in the here-and-now have given rise to the patient's misinterpretation that he is rejecting, especially when there has been a sudden switch in the patient's attitude in the way indicated above. Very often, some quite trivial alteration in his behaviour may trigger off feelings of rejection. For example, a patient may say: 'You didn't smile when you opened the door for me'; or, 'Your voice sounded different. I was sure that you were fed up with me'; or 'You yawned whilst I was talking'.

Although psychotherapists must try to remain calmly and reliably the same, their demeanour is bound to vary from day to day to a minor degree. Perhaps the therapist is tired or worried or has a hang-over. Patients who are hyper-sensitive to rejection pick on changes in the therapist's behaviour which may be trivial, but which, nonetheless, are really there. It is therefore unwise to dismiss the patient's complaints as having no basis at all in reality. Although, as I have explained, there are very good reasons why the therapist should not talk about his own feelings, there is no reason why he should not admit to being human without going into details. Thus, in response to the patient's accusation that he is 'different', he might say: 'Yes, I expect I do vary from time to time just as you do. One has to allow for that in other people. I wonder why you find it so difficult to tolerate.'

If the therapist has really been at fault; that is, if he has actually yawned, or missed something the patient was saying, or forgotten something which the patient told him previously, he must always admit it. Psychotherapy can only be conducted on the basis of honesty on both sides, and to pretend to be better than one is is to falsify the relationship.

Provided the therapist has the fortitude and tact to hold on through the times during which the patient accuses him of lack of understanding, the patient's 'good' image of him will predominate. However, depending upon the degree of disturbance shown by the patient, this image will tend to be idealised in the way already hinted at. That is, the therapist will be seen as impossibly good, understanding, loving; a paragon of all the virtues, an idealised parent who will solve all problems, heal all hurts, make up for past unhappiness. What the patient is seeking from the therapist is total devotion of a kind which only new-born babies are justified in expecting. It is extremely difficult to obtain objective evidence of what has actually been missing in the patient's early development to account for this infantile demand; but, in a few instances, I have been given evidence that the patient's mother was actually incapable of loving her children. It has often seemed to me that, if human beings have not been given what they need at the appropriate stage in their development, they are left with a compulsive hunger which drives them to try and obtain what has been missing. Whether this is actually true or not, this explanation helps me to understand the kind of patient I have been attempting to describe. He or she is driven to demand from the therapist the total acceptance, protection, care and love which mothers give their new-born infants at the stage when nothing can be expected from the infant in return.

The therapist cannot, of course, fulfil such an unrealistic expectation. Even if he were to abandon all his other work, and take up residence with the patient, be available at any hour of the day, minister to the patient's slightest requirement, he still could not make up for the past nor wholly fill the aching void which the patient carries inside. Such patients have to come to terms with the fact that, although the therapist may have been able to help them to make a new and better kind of relationship with the people they encounter, he cannot wholly replace what has been missing in early childhood. To accept this is exactly like coming to terms with a physical disability. If one has lost a leg, one has to make do with an artificial substitute. If the patient can accept this, the compulsive demands cease, and the patient comes to look at other people in a new and more realistic light. It is, perhaps, a matter of being able to allow oneself to be depressed; to mourn for the ideal mother who never was, rather than continue to hope to find her in someone else.

In my view, hysteria is best regarded in the light of a defence against depression. In trying to avoid pain the patient makes things worse rather than better. It is only when the therapist has an appreciation of what lies behind the hysterical façade that he can help such patients.

Reference

1. Nicholi, Armand M. (ed.) (1978) *The Harvard Guide to Modern Psychiatry*, p. 287. Cambridge, Massachusetts: The Belknap Press, Harvard University Press.

10

The Depressive Personality

Depression is probably the commonest symptom which brings a patient to see a psychiatrist. It may range in severity from a temporary state of low morale which anyone is likely to experience in the face of commonplace setbacks, to a tormenting condition of melancholic hopelessness which may result in suicide. In the past, psychiatrists were wont to divide depression into 'neurotic' and 'psychotic' varieties. The former was often called 'reactive'; a term which implied that the patient's state was clearly a response, though perhaps an excessive response, to definable events like bereavement, a broken love affair, failure in an examination, loss of a job or a financial reverse. Cases of 'reactive' depression were sometimes treated with drugs or ECT; or might be referred to the psychotherapist, especially if other neurotic symptoms accompanied the depression. Psychotic varieties of depression, on the other hand, were referred to as 'endogenous'; that is, as taking origin from the patient's personality without reference to external events. Such cases of depression were more likely to be accompanied by insomnia, loss of appetite and consequent loss of weight, and other physiological manifestations of disorder. Faced with a patient of this kind, most psychiatrists were, and are, content to prescribe anti-depressant drugs or electrically-induced convulsions without feeling it their duty to investigate the patient's personal psychology or social circumstances in any detail.

Although it remains true that the more profound varieties of depression are best treated with drugs or ECT, this is because those who are suffering from very severe depression are incapable of that minimum degree of rapport and co-operation without which the psychotherapist is helpless. It is almost certainly not because their disorder is of a different kind from that milder variety which is labelled 'neurotic' or 'reactive'. There does not seem to be any clear division between the two. Instead, depression, like pain, seems to vary along a scale of intensity. The difference between the varieties of depression is not intrinsic, but a matter of degree.

Moreover, research has shown that social factors play a far greater part in determining whether or not a commonplace 'traumatic' event produces clinically definable depression or not. Research carried out by Professor George Brown and his associates has demonstrated that depression seldom comes out of the blue without any precipitant, and women who react to traumatic events with depression are generally contending with a variety of difficulties which render this response more probable. Thus, women who are struggling with an unsatisfactory marriage or with poor housing are more likely to become depressed. So are women who lost their mother before the age of eleven. Other factors which render them more vulnerable are having three or more children under the age of fourteen at home; having no other adult in whom to confide; and having no employment outside the home. Working-class women are four times as likely to become depressed in response to precipitating events as are their middle-class counterparts.[1] Those who have to cope with chronic physical ill-health are also more vulnerable to depression; and in underdeveloped countries, chronic depression is common as the result of malnutrition, disease, and infestation with parasites. In our own culture, certain infections, for example glandular fever and influenza, are notorious for leaving the sufferer depressed, as are the biochemical changes which follow upon the end of pregnancy, or which occur at the menopause. Pre-menstrual tension and depression are sometimes associated.

It is, therefore, extremely important that the psychiatrist takes into account all the circumstances of the patient's life, both past and present, if he is to understand the condition. In addition, he must, I believe, learn to understand the personality of those who are particularly liable to depression, even if he believes that this liability is primarily caused by genetic factors rather than by adverse circumstances.

People who are particularly liable to become depressed are said to have 'depressive personalities', or to exhibit 'depressive psychopathology'. Patients of this kind make up a considerable part of any psychotherapeutic practice. The picture is complicated by the fact that depressive personalities are not all of one kind. There is reason to believe that the so-called 'bipolar' manic-depressive, who tends to swing in mood from one extreme to the other, has fewer neurotic traits than those people who suffer only from depression. Some of those who are temperamentally inclined toward depression are, except when actually suffering from the condition, robust, aggressive personalities who, most of the time, cope successfully with their underlying tendency by being overactive. Balzac and Winston Churchill were both examples of this type. However, most of the depressives who come the way of the psychotherapist belong to a more passive, dependent group; and it is this variety of person whom I shall discuss in most detail.

In the face of adversity, people with this kind of personality tend to feel both helpless and hopeless. Instead of imagining that, by their own efforts, they can improve their condition, they believe themselves to be at the mercy of events. On the surface, they may display not only misery, but hopeless resignation, affirming that whatever adverse circumstance is making them depressed was not only to be expected, but also, in some way, their own fault. Their resignation is more apparent than real; for, like the rest of mankind, they not only suffer, but also resent what has caused their suffering, However, instead of their resentment being mobilised to make an effective 'aggressive' response, it is repressed and turned inward, showing itself only in self-blame and self-depreciation.

Depressives, therefore, present themselves as far more ineffective and inadequate than in fact they are; and the psychotherapist's task is not only to reinforce the glimmer of hope which has brought the patient to seek help, but also to disinter the active, aggressive aspect of his personality which, being largely repressed, is unavailable to him.

Depressives of this variety often obtain considerable benefit from psychotherapy. Although modern anti-depressant drugs have brought relief to many of those suffering from severe attacks of depression, there is no doubt that, at the time of writing, these drugs are grossly over-prescribed, and may also have had the effect of deterring some of those who would benefit from psychotherapy from seeking it. Learning to cope more effectively with life and with one's own temperament will not be brought about by drugs; and although temporary alleviation of depression can be effected by their prescription, continued long-term use is seldom justified, and may actually be harmful, since it tends to blunt the patient's sensibilities, and prevent him from coming to terms with reality.

I do not claim, as some analysts tend to, that the tendency to become depressed in response to adversity can, in all cases, be entirely abolished; but rather to affirm that particular episodes of depression can be alleviated, and that the patient can be helped to deal better with depression should it recur.

In my view, the most striking characteristic of depressives is a negative one; an absence of built-in self-esteem. When a person is actually suffering from depression, it is usual for him to feel, and to refer to himself as, worthless, no good, hopeless, not worth bothering with, a failure and so on. Such expressions are of course determined by internal, rather than external factors. Although the patient's depression may have been initiated by one of the events already referred to above (bereavement, a broken love affair etc.), his feelings of hopelessness and his self-castigation seem to the observer to be out of proportion to the event which sparked them off. The respiratory tract of an asthmatic is unduly sensitive to certain allergens which cause a degree of bronchial spasm and outpouring of mucus comparable to that induced in a normal person by poison gas. The psyche of the depressive is unduly sensitive to events which lower self-esteem, reacting profoundly to reverses which, to the normal person, seem trivial. Thus, a quarrel with someone emotionally important which, to the ordinary person, seems no more than a passing episode, seems to the depressive to be the end of the world. Failure in an examination which, to most schoolchildren or undergraduates, would involve no more than a transient annoyance at having to repeat some work may, in the depressive, spark off a reaction involving feelings of total

97

worthlessness. Depressives often take the view that, in their periods of depression, they have greater insight into the true nature of things than when they are cheerful. They sometimes opine that periods of freedom from depression are no more than mirages which obscure reality. Most psychiatrists take the opposite view, believing that the patient's depressed mood distorts his vision. However, there is a sense in which the patient is right. As we shall see, a great part of the depressive person's life is determined by his efforts to avoid depression; to establish defences against this dread condition by overactivity, gaining esteem from external sources, or any other manoeuvre which will prevent descent into the abyss. It seems that the state of depression is a constant which underlies all the fronts which he may present to the world in rather the same way that a house may be in a sad state of decay though presenting a brightly-painted exterior. Although the depressive's protestations of his own worthlessness may seem exaggerated, he is right when he affirms that his state of depression is more real, more truly reflective of his essential self, than his state of mind at other times: it is so for him, however it may seem to anyone else.

From what source is self-esteem derived, and why is it that the depressive has so little of it? No-one knows the complete answer to either of these questions, but it is possible to give a partial explanation which is an approximation to the truth in many instances.

The human infant is born into the world in a peculiarly helpless and dependent state, and remains at least partially helpless and dependent for a period which, in comparison with his total life-span, is longer than that of any other animal. It is reasonable to assume that the human infant has, at first, but little notion of his own capabilities or lack of them. As he matures, however, he becomes increasingly aware of his dependency and helplessness relative to adults. If he is brought up in a home in which he is welcomed, played with, cuddled, and generally 'made much of', the likelihood is that he will come to feel himself sufficiently a worthwhile person to counteract his realisation of his own inevitable inadequacy compared with adults. One could equally well say, in the jargon of psychologists, that repeated positive reinforcement has conditioned him to favourable self-appraisal; or in Kleinian terminology, that he has introjected his parents as 'good objects'. Loved children are generally praised for every new accomplishment; for every word learned, for the beginnings of manual skills, for all kinds of achievements which, only a year or two later, will be taken for granted. And the more that parents are irrationally adoring, the more is a child likely to grow up thinking well of himself, even if his actual achievements are extremely modest. In the sentence above, I put the words 'made much of' into inverted commas deliberately to draw attention to the fact that loving parents habitually, and rightly, overvalue everything that their infants do. Because his parents value him so highly, the child comes to have a good opinion of himself. Whereas his self-esteem originally depended upon repeated affirmations of his worth from outside sources, it eventually comes to depend upon something within himself which has become 'built-in' as part of his own personality. The process is similar to that of the formulation of conscience, in which prohibitions originally promulgated by parents become the person's own conscience or super-ego.

Contact with the mother may be interrupted by her illness or death. Research into the development of subhuman primates has confirmed the hypothesis that some forms of depression may be related to severance of the mother-child tie in infancy. Monkey infants brought up in isolation for six months are fearful and insecure when introduced to their peers; are unable to play; and, later, are unable to mate. Infant monkeys which are separated from their mothers for short periods even when they have already become somewhat independent not only become depressed at the time, but show after-effects which persist for years, for example, less social play and greater fear of strange objects. Suppose, however, that something in the parent-child relation goes wrong. Parents may not proffer enough irrational adoration; or may tend to keep the child over-dependent, thus depriving him of any sense of his own achievement. A child may be born with a physical disability, or may suffer so much ill-health that he continues to feel inadequate compared with his peers. Or the parents may set such high standards that the child comes to feel that he will inevitably fail to live up to them. Depressives do not feel disregarded, as do the hysterics we discussed in the previous chapter, but rather that they have been scrupulously regarded, weighed in the balance, and found wanting.

The absence of an inner sense of worth has a number of consequences. First, such a person has a proclivity to be more than usually dependent upon the good opinion of his fellows. It is impossible for the depressive to be indifferent to what others think of him, since repeated assurance of their good opinion is as necessary to his psychic health as are repeated feeds of milk to the physical well-being of infants. Whether or not one subscribes to Freudian theory in regarding depressive personalities as being fixated at the 'oral' stage (and there is some evidence to support such an assertion; see Fisher and Greenberg[2]), there is no doubt that such personalities are 'hungry' for approval, and need recurrent proofs of their acceptability in the shape of repeated reassurance from others, recurrent successes, or other bolstering devices to prevent them relapsing into the underlying sense of despair against which they have to protect themselves. Being so dependent upon the good opinion of others and so vulnerable to criticism often has the consequence that the depressive is less than normally assertive with other people, and overanxious to please them. Whereas the hysteric, who is also overanxious to please, tends to do so in ways which are designed to elicit attention, and which are sometimes exaggerated or irritating, the depressive tends to be less obtrusively demanding. Some depressives become expert at identifying themselves with others, and are exceedingly sensitive to what the other person is feeling. Because they are so anxious to avoid blame, and to obtain approval, they develop antennae which tell them what might upset, and what might please, those with whom they are associated. This kind of sensitivity is not unlike that demanded of their secretaries by overburdened executives, who expect that they shall know, without being told, exactly in what mood the boss may be, and treat him accordingly.

This kind of adaptation to others carries with it obvious disadvantages. If a person is frightened of asserting his own opinion for fear of offending, it is not likely that he will be an effective executive or leader. The habit of deferring goes hand-in-hand with a kind of passivity which, though it may earn commendation for 'niceness', does not command respect. It can be looked upon as a prolongation of one aspect of childhood.

Children defer to their parents because they need to in order to keep their parents' approval; and also because, for many years during which they are growing up, the parents do in fact 'know better' because of their longer experience. Depressives often defer to persons who, in reality, are their inferiors; and this habitual mode of behaviour has the effect of reinforcing their sense of their own worthlessness.

Moreover, habitually to be so orientated to what the other person is feeling often has the effect of making the depressive uncertain of his own feelings; of dissociating him from his own 'inner self'. Since he is always guided by the opinions of others, he ends up by having no identifiable opinions of his own. Since he is always adapting to the emotional state of others, he becomes progressively less conscious of what he himself is feeling.

Because of their habitual suppression or repression of the independent, executive aspect of their personalities, depressives feel themselves to be, and sometimes are, more helpless than the average person, and turn to others to tell them what to do in any situation in life requiring decision. An underlying conviction that whatever choice they themselves make is likely to be wrong, and a desire to avoid blame if things in fact turn out badly, supports this tendency; with the consequence that depressives not only feel themselves helpless, but often are so in reality.

Recent work has emphasised the role of helplessness in depression. Experiment has shown that dogs, faced with unpredictable, repeated traumas in the shape of electric shocks which they cannot avoid, give up trying to escape or do anything, and simply lie down and whine.[3] Helplessness and hopelessness march hand in hand. Depressives feel themselves to be powerless to affect the course of events, and therefore 'give up' and adopt a passive role. In the histories of depressive patients, it sometimes emerges that the individual did far less well at school or university than his intellectual gifts would warrant. This is generally because, at some point in his development, he became convinced that his own efforts would be useless. Gifted persons of depressive temperament often do well when all that is required is an effortlessly clever response to material which is fed to them. They do less well when effort is required to master a subject; since they have no confidence that anything which they have to do themselves by effort is likely to be successful.

Later in life, when experience has taught them that some measure of success does in fact follow from their own efforts, they may substitute ceaseless striving for passivity. This is why achievement of a goal is often succeeded by depression. The writer who completes a book, the business man who brings off a deal, the person who is given promotion, may all find that depression rather than euphoria follows their success. This is because the aftermath of success is 'relaxation' and inactivity; to the normal person, a chance to 'recharge batteries'; to the depressive, a relapse into the conviction of his own ineffectiveness. If one has been striving very hard to achieve a particular end, completion of the task actually involves a loss; a loss of the endeavour to which so much energy has been devoted, and which, during the effort, may have contributed to self-esteem by making the individual feel effective or important. Normal people feel the need of a holiday on completion of a demanding task; depressives often find that holidays precipitate depression.

We have seen that, in their personal relationships, depressives tend to suppress their own opinions, defer to the other person, and identify with the other in order to fit in with his attitudes. This lack of assertiveness involves considerable repression of what may be called the aggressive side of the depressive's personality.

As I have pointed out elsewhere (*Human Aggression*[4] and *Human Destructiveness*[5]) it is impossible entirely to separate the violent, destructive, hostile aspect of aggression from the constructive, effective, assertive aspect, without which no decisions would be taken, no leadership proffered, no action to alter events embarked upon. Without a certain assertion of his own personality, a person ceases to exist as definably distinct. In fact, when we loosely affirm that a man or woman has 'a lot of personality', what we usually mean is that he or she is notably assertive. In his relationships with others, the depressive personality generally feels defeated. What he is usually quite unaware of is that there is another side to his masochistic submission of self; a violent, hostile and destructive side of which he is usually so frightened that he has erected formidable defences to make sure that it does not emerge. No human being can experience repeated defeats at the hands of others without resenting them. What the depressive has done, albeit automatically and without conscious intent, is to throw the baby out with the bath-water. By repressing his destructive hostility, he has at the same time deprived himself of those positive features of aggression which would allow him to assert himself when necessary, stand up to other people, initiate effective action, 'attack' difficult problems, and make his mark upon the world. I said that helplessness and hopelessness march hand in hand: let us add hostility to make a triad of 'h's.

This is not a feature of the depressive's personality which impresses itself upon the uninformed observer. To him, many depressive people appear as particularly 'nice', largely because, as we have seen, they are expert at reinforcing the personality of the other at the expense of their own. After an encounter with such a person, the other party may feel that he does not know much about the depressive person, or that he is something of an enigma or a pleasant nonentity. But most people are so pleased to have their own opinions listened to, their own views acceded respect, and their own wishes anticipated, that their feeling of warmth toward the depressive outweighs any doubts they may have about what he may 'really' be like. This is, of course, exactly what the depressive is, unconsciously, aiming at. Having abandoned hope of being effective or being thought to be so, he has fallen back on being thought 'nice' as the only way in which he can maintain his self-esteem. This niceness masks considerable hostility.

I once worked in a house in Harley Street in which the door was opened, and appointments made, by a butler of an old-fashioned variety seldom encountered today. As befitted his office, he was extremely polite, attentive, and, on occasion, even embarrassingly subservient. Patients often commented upon how 'nice' he was. However, I was aware of a very different side of his personality. My room was above his living quarters; and, after he had gone off duty, the sounds of his angry quarrels with his wife came through the floorboards. No doubt he was taking out on her the feelings of resentment toward the people to whom during his working day, he was compelled to be subservient. His 'niceness' masked considerable vindictiveness.

I have written at some length about the passive, dependent type of depressive personality because this is the type which the psychotherapist is most likely to encounter. If the view of the depressive's psychopathology which I have outlined is accepted, it is possible to outline what the therapist is aiming at with such a person, and also to suggest how positive results may be achieved. First, the fact that the therapist is willing to continue to see a depressive patient over a period of time reinforces hope and counteracts despair. Second, the therapist's acceptance and understanding of the patient tends to counteract the latter's negative view of himself, and may, if the period of therapy continues for long enough, become 'built-in' in the way described in the chapter on transference. The patient, because he comes to feel that there is at least one person in the world who genuinely appreciates him, may alter his attitude towards others, assuming, for example, that they are more likely to be friendly than critical. Third, the therapist may be able to counteract the depressive's negative view of his own accomplishments and effectiveness by drawing attention to the many occasions on which he has behaved intelligently and competently. Fourth, the therapist will try to uncover and mobilise the aggressive side of the patient's personality in order that he may be able to 'attack' life more successfully.

The psychotherapist who undertakes the treatment of persons with an underlying depressive psychopathology may find it helpful to bear in mind the following considerations. First, nearly all episodes of depression resolve themselves 'spontaneously'. I put the word 'spontaneously' into inverted commas, because close examination of such recoveries usually discloses psychological factors of a more or less subtle kind which have prompted recovery, just as close examination discloses precipitants of the attack. These factors seem to be of three kinds. First, the patient, especially if he is managing to remain at work, may find that his self-esteem is partially restored by discovering that he can be effective at it. Most jobs require repeated actions of some kind which do not demand weighty decisions or new initiatives; and the fact that a depressed person finds to his surprise that he can continue to function effectively at this level may convince him that he is not entirely useless. This is why I seldom reinforce a depressed person's desire to 'give up' and retire to bed or to hospital unless he is exhibiting clear-cut psychotic symptoms, is dangerously suicidal, or is so depressed that he cannot co-operate.

Second, a depressed person may recover because he has been able to re-establish a loving relationship with a person who is emotionally important to him. Vulnerable depressives, as I have already mentioned, may be thrown into a state of profound despair by the kind of transient quarrel which we all may have with people who love us and whom we love. The depressive has no certitude that he is worthy of love or that love will last. Its temporary disappearance is, to him, a confirmation of his pessimistic convictions. However, if a tactful spouse or other loved person manages to convince him that he is still loved, or if, more importantly, he manages to admit that he too was angry, his depression will often lift. Recovery of this kind is likely to be short-lived, and to be misinterpreted by the psychotherapist, who may flatter himself that it is the consequence of his ministrations when, in truth, it may have very little to do with them. It also may mean that the patient breaks off treatment prematurely, before the therapist has had time to do as much as he could for him. For reasons already discussed, I do not urge therapy upon those who do not want it, but I do sometimes point out that whilst recovery from depression is usual, what we want to achieve is that relapses shall be less frequent or less severe; and that learning how to deal with such episodes more effectively takes time and patience.

In the psychotherapy of depressives, it is important not to be misled by the patient's account of his own lack of effectiveness. Many such patients omit any account of the occasions when they are, or have been effective; and it is valuable to be able to elicit these and to draw attention to them. It is equally important to be able to detect when the patient has given up prematurely because he has an inner conviction that his own efforts are unlikely to bring any reward. Some depressives have a quite unrealistic picture of successful people, believing that they have acquired skills or achieved eminence without needing to apply themselves. This picture is the consequence of the depressive's childhood conviction that he can never 'measure up' to parents or other adults. I once knew a depressive who made a habit of saying of himself, 'Of course, I'm so dim'. Intellectually, he was far from dim, and in fact performed competently at a fairly high-level job; but his reiteration of his 'dimness' provided him with an excuse for less achievement than might reasonably have been expected of a man of his gifts. After all, he had always told us of it. Because of his dependency, passivity, and anxiety to please, the type of depressive patient who is generally referred for psychotherapy will quickly form a positive transference. Or rather, he will rapidly *appear* to do so, for such patients seem to be more compliant and grateful than actually they are. Psychotherapists are easily deceived into thinking that such a patient has accepted an interpretation when, in fact, he may disagree or have reservations which he does not yet dare to express. It is particularly important for the therapist to be alert to this possibility, and to interpret excessive politeness, deference and over-eager compliance with the therapist's remarks. One lesson which it is vital that the patient should learn is that it is possible to be quite different from other persons and yet retain friendly relations with them. As I said earlier, a certain amount of aggression is required to maintain differentiation of oneself as a separate entity.

The most difficult task which the therapist has with such a patient is to make him aware of his hostility. And yet it is by means of the disinterment and expression of this that recovery comes. Since the depressive adaptation almost certainly began in childhood, it will be particularly difficult to uncover and to help the patient to accept hostile emotions to his parents, whom he is likely to have idealised. A child who is a poor mixer and who cannot stand up for himself is prone to idealisation since he may feel that his parents are the only persons in the world who care for him, and that his very existence depends upon maintaining an image of them as 'perfect'. The persistence of such a belief in adult life impairs the patient's capacity to achieve independence and make new relationships.

One opportunity for disinterring hostility is when the therapist goes on holiday, or unavoidably has to cancel an appointment. The more dependent the patient is, the more will he resent being abandoned. His depression is likely to increase whilst the therapist is absent, and he will probably complain of this whilst carefully refraining from criticising the therapist in any way for leaving him. But his complaints are likely to be phrased in such a way that criticism of the therapist is implicit, for instance by employing a querulous tone of voice. Or else the patient may fall silent, saying that he has nothing to say, or that therapy is useless. This is a form of 'sulking', and if the patient can be brought to see this, he will be one step on the way to discovering that hostility can be expressed without his relationship with the therapist being terminated.

One patient who had developed techniques of deference, compliance, and an extraordinary capacity for identifying with the other person, had done so early in childhood to avoid upsetting her father, who was a difficult and bad-tempered man whose wrath, she felt, had at all costs to be avoided. Everyone who knew her liked her; and she acted as confidant and sympathiser to nearly all her friends. The consequence was that she became depressed, because she felt that her friends were imposing upon her, swamping her, and depriving her of any chance of asserting her own personality. Her way of dealing with this was to retreat from personal involvement altogether, give up her regular job, at which she was very good, and try to express herself through writing. But writing is a lonely occupation, and her dependent needs soon forced her to enter into relationships again with the consequence that she again began to feel annihilated and depressed. Her depression was really due to her feelings of resentment against those who imposed upon her and exploited her; and her problem was to recognise and express this resentment, whilst at the same time coming to understand how she herself invited exploitation.

It might be said that such a patient was not primarily depressive, but schizoid, in that she presented the typical schizoid dilemma in which closeness to others presents danger, whilst avoidance involves isolation. However, as we shall see, schizoid people lack the capacity for identification with others possessed by depressives; and, although this patient tried to isolate herself for part of the day, she was never so lonely nor so afraid of other people as are most of those whom we label schizoid.

Her attempts to become a writer draw attention to the fact that creative people sometimes have depressive psychopathology, as I have attempted to show in my book *The Dynamics of Creation.*[6] Writing and other creative pursuits may help the depressive in two ways. First, he may gain an increased sense of his own competence in being able to produce anything at all. Second, if what he produces is published or displayed, and becomes accepted by others, he will receive a boost to his self-esteem which may be repeated each time he produces something new, although, as I pointed out earlier, depression is sometimes an immediate aftermath of completing a piece of work. Depressive personalities are, as one might expect, particularly vulnerable to criticism. All creative people identify themselves to some extent with what they produce, for every piece of work, even if it consists of mathematics or observations requiring maximum scientific detachment, contains part of themselves. Imaginative writers are, as one might expect even more identified with their work than are scientists, and therefore even more sensitive about it. One of the commonest causes of 'creative block', that is, inability to conclude original work which has been embarked upon, is fear of hostile criticism when it is finally exposed. Virginia Woolf is one example of a successful writer who remained intensely vulnerable to criticism throughout her life. She had a number of attacks of depression of psychotic intensity, and finally, realising that another attack .was imminent, committed suicide.

The risk that a depressed patient may commit suicide is something which may haunt the psychotherapist, particularly if he is inexperienced. Patients of mine have done so, and I have felt guilty and depressed myself on this account. As after any bereavement, one searches one's mind for occasions where one may have said the wrong thing or failed the dead person in any way. However, I cannot recall any patient of mine taking his or her life whilst actually in regular treatment; and, from discussions with colleagues, I believe this to be rare. That is, when regular psychotherapeutic sessions have been established, and there has been time for some positive rapport to have been achieved, it is uncommon for a patient, however depressed at the end of one particular session, to feel so hopeless that the possibility of relief at the next session is entirely abandoned. The position is different if, as I recall in one example, the patient had had to discontinue treatment because of moving elsewhere; or in cases where the therapist has seen the patient only once or twice and therefore has not had time to establish a relationship. If psychotherapy is to achieve one of its main objects, that is, that the patient shall become more independent and autonomous, the risk of suicide has sometimes to be taken. At an initial consultation, if the therapist feels that suicide is an imminent possibility, he may decide that he cannot take on the case, and take steps to ensure that the patient is admitted to hospital, or treated by some other means than psychotherapy. But if the patient is coming regularly, and a psychotherapeutic relationship has been established, it is inappropriate and harmful to the patient if the therapist suddenly changes from a person who is encouraging independence and freedom of choice into a doctor with special powers to confine people in mental hospitals, against their will. It is also inadvisable for psychotherapists to prescribe anti-depressant drugs or give electroconvulsive therapy themselves since to do so means adopting a quite different role vis-à-vis the patient, and, if the patient seeks psychotherapy at a later date, when his acute disturbance has subsided, may complicate his relationship with the therapist. If a patient is deeply bent upon suicide, confining him will not necessarily prevent him from doing so. Patients who threaten suicide must be taken seriously. The idea that those who talk about suicide do not commit the act has been proven false. But it is legitimate to try and discover what lies behind the threat in the case of patients in psychotherapy. Some may be blackmailing the therapist into giving them more time, or trying to convince him that their troubles must be taken more seriously. Most such patients belong more to the category of the hysterical personalities discussed in the last chapter than to the group of seriously depressed patients. Some are seeking revenge upon those they feel have not loved them; and it is important to seek out and make conscious the hostile motive in suicide, which is almost always present. Others may be seeking oblivion, which often seems to represent a final wish for complete merging with an idealised mother of the kind portrayed by Swinburne in 'The Garden of Proserpine', where 'Even the weariest river, winds somewhere safe to sea'. It is often appropriate gently to point out that, if the patient really wants to take his own life, no-one can stop him: but that one may wonder why, if he is so determined to make an end of himself, he is bothering to tell the therapist about it or seek treatment for his condition at all. This must be done extremely tactfully, for there is a risk that the patient will take such an enquiry as a proof that the therapist does not appreciate the seriousness of his condition, and that only a suicidal attempt will bring it home to him. When I was in training, a patient of whom I had been partially in charge took an overdose after telephoning the consultant in charge of her case to ask for an urgent appointment or make some such demand, which was refused with, I believe some lack of tact, since the consultant was a notably difficult and aggressive woman herself. The patient responded by taking the seven three-grain capsules of sodium amytal with which she had been furnished on leaving the ward in the hospital to become an outpatient. This was clearly a gesture rather than a seriously intended attempt at suicide; but she developed pneumonia and died, nevertheless.

Such cases, fortunately, are rare; and I reiterate that suicide seldom occurs during the course of psychotherapy, provided there has been time for rapport to be established. An inexperienced psychotherapist may feel the need to urge the patient to see a more senior colleague in cases in which he is seriously worried about the possibility of suicide. In this instance, he will be wise to explain to the patient exactly why he advises this course, and leave it to him to follow it or not as he wishes. In most instances, the patient will not want to see somebody else, and will refuse to do so. Since this is an assertion of his independence, his refusal must be accepted. The therapist will discover that, at the next session, much useful material will probably emerge which will be concerned with how genuine is the patient's wish to die, and with how competent or not he believes the therapist to be. A number of people with an underlying depressive psychopathology manage to avoid becoming clinically depressed by over-work or by finding legitimate enemies upon whom to vent their aggression. When such manoeuvres are overdone to the extent to which they become obvious to the layman, it is common for psychiatrists to refer to the patient as employing a 'manic defence'. An example of such a person is Winston Churchill.[7] Churchill became depressed when he was immobilised, as during his brief imprisonment by the Boers; or when confronted by certain failures, as in the case of the campaign which he initiated in the Dardanelles during the 1914–18 War. His background gave ample reason why he should be vulnerable to what he called his 'Black Dog'. But, during most of his life he was adept at staving off depression. Whilst he was awake he was seldom idle, and when he stopped working he went to bed (albeit at 3 a.m.) rather than 'relaxing'. He had, for much of his life, the sustaining influence of holding great office. When he was out of office, he turned to painting, a creative activity which he himself describes in notably aggressive terms. He was at his best during the 1939–45 War in which Hitler was so legitimate an enemy that few people doubted the necessity of defeating him. Churchill admirably dealt with his underlying psychopathology until old age and arteriosclerosis undermined his will and he relapsed into what appears to have been a kind of depressive stupor during his closing years. No-one could be less like the passive, dependent type of depressive; nor more improbably a psychiatric patient than Churchill. But the psychotherapist will have referred to him a number of people, including politicians, whose defences against depression are of similar type, and who are far from being dependent or passive.

John Stuart Mill provides a good example of a man who suffered a severe attack of depression in adult life whose up-bringing clearly predisposed him to this happening. As many people will remember, John Stuart Mill was remarkable in his intellectual precocity. His father, James Mill, himself under-took his education, with the consequence that Mill started to learn Greek at three years old, and, by the time he was eight, he had read the whole of Herodotus, Xenophon's *Cyropaedia*, the first six dialogues of Plato, and much else besides. He records that it was 'totally impossible' that he should have understood the Theaetetus of Plato. 'But my father, in all his teaching, demanded of me not only the utmost that I could do, but much that I could by no possibility have done.' Although Mill, by his own reckoning, started with an advantage of a quarter of a century over his contemporaries because of his father's rigorous educational methods, he was so kept from mixing with them that he had no idea, until he was over fourteen, that his achievements were in any way remarkable. Measuring himself against his father, he had always found himself to be wanting. Moreover, since he had been so carefully segregated and had not participated in games or in the ordinary pursuits of boys, his physical skills were minimal, and he remained 'inexpert in anything requiring manual dexterity'. Far ahead in intellectual matters, 'The deficiencies in my education were principally in the things which boys learn from being turned out to shift for themselves, and from being brought together in large numbers'. Moreover, Mill's father was a man of exceptional energy and decision, and, as Mill observed: 'The children of energetic parents frequently grow up unenergetic, because they lean on their parents, and the parents are energetic for them'.

This is not the place to describe the depression which so deeply afflicted Mill when he was twenty years old, though every psychiatrist ought to read his own account of it. It must suffice to mention that the first ray of light broke in upon his gloom when he was reading some memoirs in which the author relates his father's death, 'the distressed position of the family, and the sudden inspiration by which he, then a mere boy, felt and made them feel that he would be everything to them – would supply the place of all that they had lost'. Mill records that he wept at this affecting account; and clearly believes that it was because the book made him able to feel emotion again that he started to improve in spirits. Another interpretation would be that this passage made him aware that sons can sometimes aspire to replace, or even surpass, their fathers; and it was this realisation which made him feel less inadequate.[8]

However this may be, Mill's upbringing clearly demonstrates that a child may receive the most devoted attention from his parents but fail to acquire a proper sense of his own value. And both Churchill's life and Mill's demonstrate that great achievements, of entirely different varieties, may in part come about because an individual who, in early life, believed himself to be inadequate, is driven to make especial efforts to prove the contrary.

References
1. Brown, George W. and Harris, Tirril (1978) *Social Origins of Depression*. London: Tavistock.
2. Fisher, Seymour and Greenberg, Roger P. (1977) *The Scientific Credibility of Freud's Theories and Therapy*, Chapter 3. New York; Basic Books.

3.   Seligman, Martin E. P. (1975) *Helplessness*. San Francisco: W. H. Freeman.

4.   Storr, Anthony (1968) *Human Aggression*. London: Allen Lane, The Penguin Press.

5.   Storr, Anthony (1972) *Human Destructiveness*. Sussex University Press.

6.   Storr, Anthony (1972) *The Dynamics of Creation*. London: Secker and Warburg.

7.   Storr, Anthony (1988) *Churchill's Black Dog, Kafka's Mice & Other Phenomena of the Human Mind*. New York: Grove Press. London: Collins (1989).

8.   Mill, John Stuart (1873) *Autobiography* pp. 5, 6, 35, 37, 141. London: Longmans, Green, Reader and Dyer.

11

The Obsessional Personality

Persons of obsessional personality are meticulous, scrupulous, accurate, reliable, honest, and much concerned with control, order, and cleanliness. Many of those who have made outstanding contributions to Western culture exhibit these traits of personality. Indeed, most people of considerable intellectual accomplishment need to be somewhat obsessional to achieve their results. Only when these traits become exaggerated into compulsive rituals or tormenting thoughts do we speak of obsessional neurosis.

Freud described his own personality as obsessional, and once said to Jung that, if he were to suffer from neurosis, it would be of the obsessional variety. He described obsessional personalities as 'noteworthy for a regular combination of the three following characteristics. They are especially *orderly, parsimonious* and *obstinate*'.[1] Found together, these traits constituted what Freud named the 'anal' character, since he believed that they took origin from the period at which the child was being taught control of his sphincters; a period at which the anal region was alleged to be the main focus of emotional concern. In Freud's view, 'Cleanliness, orderliness and trustworthiness give exactly the impression of a reaction–formation against an interest in what is unclean and disturbing and should not be part of the body. ("Dirt is matter in the wrong place.")'[2]

Obstinacy may first be manifested in the child's refusal to

excrete in the right place at the right time as indicated by those in authority. Parsimony arises because of a peculiar connection between money and faeces; the phrase 'filthy lucre' being one example of such a connection. Today, we think of parsimony in more general terms, as a reluctance to part with bodily contents or with anything that is felt intimately to belong to the self.

Research designed to discover whether obsessional neurosis and 'anal' traits of character are the consequence of harsh toilet-training or of particular conflicts during the period of acquiring sphincter control has not found any causal connection. But Freud's description of the anal character, and his perception that certain traits are habitually associated together, are accurate. Some of Freud's theoretical explanations have been discredited, but he remains a great clinical observer.

Some people with obsessional personalities are prone to develop obsessional, compulsive symptoms. These take the form of unwanted thoughts which intrude upon the patient's consciousness; or of ritual actions which the patient feels compelled to carry out against his will. The line between pathology and normality is often hard to draw. If a man exhibits occasional anxiety as to whether he has closed his front door or turned off the gas taps, we disregard his doubts, for we have probably experienced the same phenomena ourselves. But if he always has to check the door and the taps ten times before he leaves the house, we label him neurotic. Writers ought to be meticulous in their choice of words; but there is something wrong with those who, like Dorothy Parker, say 'I can't write five words but that I change seven.'[3] However, the majority of obsessional patients who come the way of the psychotherapist exhibit traits and behaviour which are not more than slight exaggerations of valuable aspects of the obsessional personality; scrupulosity, reliability, self-control, and honesty. They seek psychotherapy because of tension and anxiety, or because of difficulties in interpersonal relationships. Such obsessive symptoms as compulsive rituals or intrusive thoughts are generally no more than minor, incidental features of their problems.

Whatever the causal origin of the 'anal', obsessional personality there can be no doubt of the emphasis which such persons put upon control and order. Like all obsessional traits, the drive toward attaining order and control is Janus-faced; that is, when present in moderation, it is valuable, indeed, essential to the more complex pursuits of civilised life. When exaggerated, it is destructive of spontaneity, and may eventually paralyse action. In previous chapters, we saw that hysterics often feel of no account, and that depressives often feel helpless and hopeless. Obsessionals actively defend themselves against such feelings, and strive to master both themselves and the external world. At the same time, they often behave as if some unspecified disaster was about to overtake them. Mastery of oneself, and to some extent of one's environment, is something which we all teach our children as desirable, and which we hope they will increasingly attain as they grow up. But we also have to accept that our control can never be complete. In the external world, accidents will happen, whether these be the minor mishaps of everyday life, or disasters on the scale of earthquakes or tornadoes. However fiercely we discipline our unruly minds and bodies, we can never entirely control ourselves. Even those who dislike the processes involved must need both to eat and excrete; and, in the case of the majority, sex is so urgent a drive that it, too, cannot be entirely subdued. Much of our mental life, from dream to inspiration, is beyond the reach of the will. We have to fit in with our own natures, just as we do with those of other people; and the idea that control over ourselves can ever be absolute is an illusion.

Most people with obsessional traits of personality are not in any sense 'ill'. Indeed, they are indispensable to Western civilisation, and thus command admiration and respect. Intellectuals, whether in the sciences or in the humanities, are commonly of obsessional personality. The philosopher Kant is a good example of a scholar whose whole life was ordered with meticulous exactness. The obsessional scholar's ideal, which can never be wholly realised, is that the world shall be an ordered place in which everything is understood and everything is predictable. Such also is the vision of the scientist. The progress of science depends upon the invention of hypotheses which, by bringing an ever-increasing number of facts into causal relation with each other and under one heading, impose order upon chaos, and enable more and more accurate predictions to be made. It is the discernment of anomalies, of facts not covered by existing hypotheses, which leads to new discoveries and new theories. Anomalies are a form of disorder which spur the scientist on to create a more comprehensive order; just as dirt or disarray may impel an obsessional to arrange and rearrange his room.

In spite of this resemblance, the sense of unrest and irritation which afflicts the scientist who observes an anomaly which does not fit existing theory cannot be labelled a neurotic symptom. Even some phenomena which are usually deemed to be obsessional rituals hardly deserve the name. Is the child who demands that his parent shall tell him the same story, arrange his bedclothes in a particular way, and kiss him goodnight in precisely the same fashion, behaving pathologically? Such ritual observances are symbolic protections against the dangers of being alone in the dark; a situation in which many children feel threatened, both from within and without. To dismiss such ritual practices as superstitious is to undervalue their significance and effectiveness. As I pointed out in *The Dynamics of Creation*,[4] rituals are often valuable to creative people as means whereby they are put in touch with their sources of inspiration, just as religious rituals serve the purpose of inducing an appropriate state of mind in the worshipper. Man is man because he uses symbols and rituals to transmute the raw stuff of instinct into intellectual and artistic creations. The fact that symbolisation and ritualisation can become exaggerated to the point at which an obsessional neurotic is dominated by them as symptoms should not blind us to their vital significance in civilised life.

We have noted that obsessional personalities are particularly concerned with order and control, both of themselves and of their environment. For them, as for the child who fears the dark, both the external world and the inner world of the mind are places of danger. Only perpetual vigilance and unrelenting discipline can ensure that neither get out of hand. In the IXth book of *The Republic* Socrates says that 'in all of us, even in good men, there is a lawless wild-beast nature, which peers out in sleep'. Obsessionals behave as if the beast was straining at the leash. Moreover, they are apt to assume that other people are similarly constituted; and therefore look on the world as a jungle in which the unseen hosts of Midian are forever on the prowl.

The wild beast which obsessionals fear is principally an aggressive animal. Although sexual impulses often constitute a part of the forces which obsessionals are trying to control, aggression plays a larger part than love in their psychology. Instead of perceiving other people as persons with whom they can make relationships on equal terms, obsessionals tend to relate in terms of domination versus submission, or superiority versus inferiority. This way of interacting with others can be interpreted as a persistence of a childhood attitude; a relic of a time in which parents, however loving, were also perceived as authorities; as caretakers who were inevitably restrictive and who might become angry unless placated. As soon as any developing child begins to come into conflict with his parents (and this conflict may be particularly acute if the parents are themselves of obsessional temperament), his attitude toward them is necessarily ambivalent; that is, a mixture of love and hate. The weaker the child feels himself to be in relation to authority, or the more dominant that authority is in fact, the more will resentment equal or outweigh the love he feels.

In his paper *The Disposition to Obsessional Neurosis*, Freud made the interesting suggestion that, in such people, emotional development and intellectual development were somehow out of phase. 'I suggest the possibility that a chronological outstripping of libidinal development by ego development should be included in the disposition to obsessional neurosis. A precocity of this kind would necessitate the choice of an object under the influence of the ego-instincts, at a time at which the sexual instincts had not yet assumed their final shape, and a fixation at the stage of the pregenital sexual organization would thus be left.'[5] This statement may not be clear to those not steeped in the technical language of psychoanalysis, so I will try to put it another way. Many, though not all, persons of obsessional disposition show precocious intellectual development in childhood. This is especially true of the type of intellectual mentioned earlier. When such a child perceives his parents as restrictive authorities, he learns to relate to them by means of his intelligence rather than emotionally. That is, he becomes intensely and precociously aware of what they are feeling, in order to placate them and avoid their displeasure. Instead of battling with them, and gradually learning to assert his own power or prove his own equality, such a child need never enter into competition. This means that he will continue to regard parents and adults in general as superior in power to himself; and it also follows that he is likely to carry with him into adult life a greater than usual quantity of resentment toward other people. For an adaptation toward others which involves treating them as if they were authorities who might suddenly become angry must necessarily involve the persistence of aggressive feelings toward them, and must also demand the exercise of considerable control over such feelings. In adult life, obsessionals tend either to be authoritarian and often irritable; or else unduly submissive. Either attitude is one in which the object is to disarm the other party. Faced with possible hostility, he either conquers or submits. In neither case can he achieve equality and mutual respect.

Obsessionals entering psychotherapy often appear to be especially mild, compliant characters who are anxious to please the therapist and who agree too readily with everything which he may propose. Fear of aggression from others dominates their adaptation to their fellows. They are usually carefully and neatly dressed, in order to forestall any possible criticism of their appearance. They are punctilious in keeping appointments for which they often arrive early. They show gratitude toward the therapist before he has had time to do anything to help them, and are overanxious about causing him any possible inconvenience. Obsessionals of this type make admirable bank clerks and secretaries. In my first psychiatric post one such secretary telephoned before completing his typing of a letter which I had dictated. Had I said 'Yours truly' or 'Yours faithfully'? I could not remember, but he was anxious to be precisely accurate. A patient exhibiting many features of this temperament told me that he paid all his bills in shops with cash. Otherwise, he might find that, whilst he wrote a cheque, he was keeping other customers waiting; a delay which might make them annoyed. This same man, whose job was to check certain lists which others compiled in the factory in which he worked, was extremely good at detecting errors. But it was torture to him to have to point out these errors to those who had perpetrated them; for he feared that they might become distressed or angry. It is this kind of person who, if one steps on his toe, apologises for causing one inconvenience. Obsessionals of this type share many characteristics with depressives, and indeed often become depressed themselves when their obsessional defences are undermined by some factor which increases their anxiety.

Whereas this variety of obsessional is primarily concerned with warding off the aggression of other people, there is another type who is more concerned with controlling his own. When his defences fail, he becomes naggingly critical, and may be extremely difficult to live with. Tense, irritable, obsessional parents who want to keep everything under tight control extend this wish to those with whom they live. They insist upon cleanliness and tidiness; upon locking doors, being polite, keeping up appearances, not offending the neighbours. For such people, living in a family is difficult. They may be able so to order their own behaviour that they have no feeling that things will 'get out of hand', but they cannot entirely control the behaviour of other people. Their anxiety leads to anger, and it is small wonder that their wives and children rebel against what they feel to be an irrational tyranny.

It is easy to see, therefore, that the obsessional person's failure to integrate or control his aggressive impulses may lead in either of two directions; toward submission, on the one hand, or toward tyranny on the other. Extreme submission leads to his virtual disappearance as a separate entity. Extreme tyranny leads to the annihilation of the other, and hence to isolation.

These observations explain how it is the obsessional

defences may be employed against both depressive and schizoid states. If the subject stays close to people, he may become angry with them because he cannot control them; or else he may turn his anger against himself and so become depressed. Alternatively, he may detach himself from people. It is possible to live with a family and remain uninvolved emotionally. This type of defence is schizoid; a retreat into isolation so that the subject cannot be affected by people. The person who is unaffected by others cannot either be angry with them or suffer their anger.

When personalities of this kind develop overt symptoms, there is usually clear evidence of aggression in their psychopathology. Compulsive, intrusive thoughts tend to be of the pattern described in Chapter 5, *Interpretation*, in which a woman was distressed by the thought that she might boil her baby. Some obsessionals cannot ascend to a high place, or even travel on top of a bus without entertaining the thought that they might drop something on passers-by. Clergymen, whose profession requires that they be more habitually kind and understanding than they can always manage, not infrequently fear that swear-words or obscenities will escape their lips at inappropriate moments, as when they are preaching. Housewives may anxiously feel compelled to put all food which they serve to their families through a sieve, in case some minute particle of glass might do someone an injury. Such symptoms represent a failure of defence in that the repressed, underlying aggression of the subject is allowed to peep through.

The psychotherapist's task with such people is twofold. First, he must facilitate the emergence of the instinctive impulses against which the patient is defending himself. Second, he must present himself as a person with whom the patient can experiment in trying to reach a new kind of relationship on more equal terms; a relation in which the question of who is dominant and who is submissive is no longer crucial.

Obsessional patients are generally described as difficult subjects for psychotherapy because of their capacity for intellectualisation. Since their whole defensive system is one designed not to allow the free expression of emotion, they find it just as hard or as dangerous to 'let go' during psychotherapy as they find it in other situations in life. If, as children, they have been precocious intellectually in the way already described, they will bring this kind of adaptation to people into the therapeutic situation. That is, they will be anxious to understand exactly what the utterances of the therapist mean. Often, they will accept his explanations of their psychology as likely to be reasonable without giving any indication that these interpretations have struck home in the kind of way which might bring about modification. Obsessionals tend to understand with their heads rather than with their hearts. Since intelligent patients of this type are often verbally fluent, they are able to use words as a way of distancing themselves from their true feelings rather than as a means of expressing their true feelings. So, when the therapist says something which might be expected to pro-duce outrage, like 'You must have wanted to *murder* your mother!' the patient mildly replies: 'Perhaps you're right. I suppose something of the kind must be involved.'

Such patients become much more accessible when they are depressed. It is often helpful to pick up any tiny instance of spontaneous reaction to the therapist in the here-and-now, since this may give access to the spontaneous feelings which the patient tries so hard to control. It is also useful to explore dreams, since these may be the quickest way of demonstrating to a patient that he has another side to his personality which he is attempting to suppress and banish. Some obsessional patients find that they can 'let go' better through the medium of painting and drawing than they can by using words.

Of all patients, obsessionals are the most likely to persist in psychotherapy even when showing little evidence of im-provement. Compliant, grateful, and hopeful – at least on the surface – they are regarded by the therapist as 'good' patients with whom he enjoys working. It is part of the obsessional's problem that he tends to live in the future rather than in the present. His habit of anticipating danger leads him to take all sorts of precautions about the future and to be preoccupied with it to the exclusion of the present. As I wrote elsewhere, obsessionals at the theatre may be so preoccupied with imagining how they are going to get home afterwards that they fail to appreciate the performance itself. The same tendency makes them able to look forward to the effects of psychotherapy in the future, without fully participating in the therapeutic relation in the present. Some of the analyses which have attracted most criticism on the grounds that they have gone on for many years represent obsessionality in both parties; in the therapist as well as in the patient.

The psychotherapist who treats obsessional patients of the kind who are suitable for psychotherapy will find them intensely interesting, but may become discouraged by their lack of immediate response. However, if he sees the relatives of such patients, he may find that he is producing more results than he is aware of. Obsessional patients do alter and improve; but because of their self-control do not necessarily show much direct evidence of this to the psychotherapist. The psychotherapist's aim is that the patient shall be able to drop his defence sufficiently for him to be spontaneous, at any rate intermittently. This is why 'here-and now' interpretations are so important. Every risk which the patient is able to take in the psychotherapeutic situation is a step forward.

Cases of obsessional personality combined with mild compulsive symptoms are suitable for psychotherapy and rewarding to treat. However, there are also cases of severe obsessive-compulsive disorder which are beyond the capacity of the psychotherapist to ameliorate, and which are so extreme as to suggest that the causal factors are not purely psychogenic. These are the patients whose lives are so dominated by rituals that they can scarcely find time for any normal living. Some patients of this kind are even more disabled than if they were suffering from the less severe forms of chronic schizophrenia.

Samuel Johnson is a telling and famous example of a person who, throughout most of his life, employed obsessional defences to control aggressive impulses and to ward off the depression which constantly threatened him. If he were to present himself for treatment today, I think it probable that most psychiatrists would want to give him anti-depressant drugs as well as psychotherapy.

There are references to Johnson's obsessional rituals and

convulsive movements scattered through Boswell's *Life of Johnson*. Many of these references, together with other contemporary descriptions of Johnson's extraordinary behaviour, can be found assembled by the neurologist, Russell Brain, in his essay *The Great Convulsionary*.[6]

Some writers have alleged that Johnson suffered from the syndrome described by Gilles de la Tourette, in which multiple tics are accompanied by coprolalia, but neurological opinion is divided. Lord Brain concluded that Johnson did not suffer from any organic disease of the nervous system, a conclusion supported by Jackson Bate, whose biography of Johnson is a model of conscientious research. Johnson's tics and obsessional habits appear to have started in about his twentieth year (Gilles de la Tourette's syndrome usually begins in childhood). Bate observes that he exhibited almost every known category of tic and compulsive gesture; but that they all had one common denominator: 'an instinctive effort to control – to control aggressions by turning them in against himself. . . . Or they were employed to control anxiety and reduce things to apparent manageability by "compartmentalization," by breaking things down into units through measurement (counting steps, touching posts, and the like), just as he turned to arithmetic, as Mrs. Thrale said, when he felt his mind disordered.'[7]

Boswell wrote: 'He had another particularity, of which none of his friends ever ventured to ask an explanation. It appeared to me some superstitious habit, which he had contracted early, and from which he had never called upon his reason to disentangle him. This was his anxious care to go out or in at a door or passage by a certain number of steps from a certain point, or at least so as that either his right or his left foot, (I am not certain which,) should constantly make the first actual movement when he came close to the door or passage. Thus I conjecture: for I have, upon innumerable occasions, observed him suddenly stop, and then seem to count his steps with a deep earnestness; and when he had neglected or gone wrong in this sort of magical movement, I have seen him go back again, put himself in a proper posture to begin the ceremony, and, having gone through it, break from his abstraction, walk briskly on, and join his companion.'[8]

Johnson's gestures and movements were particularly evident when his attention was not engaged, but he could control them when he had to do so. Sir Joshua Reynolds, to whom Johnson sat for his portrait, wrote to Boswell: 'Those motions or tricks of Dr. Johnson are improperly called convulsions. He could sit motionless, when he was told to do so, as well as any other man; my opinion is that it proceeded from a habit which he had indulged himself in, of accompanying his thoughts with certain untoward actions, and those actions always appeared to me as if they were meant to reprobate some part of his past conduct. Whenever he was not engaged in conversation, such thoughts were sure to rush into his mind; and, for this reason, any company, any employment whatever, he preferred to being alone. The great business of his life (he said) was to escape from himself; this disposition he considered as the disease of his mind, which nothing cured but company.'[9] Lord Brain quotes Miss Reynolds as writing: 'He seemed to struggle almost incessantly with some mental evil, and often, by the expression of his countenance and the motion of his lips appeared to be offering up some ejaculation to Heaven to remove it.'[10]

These clinical descriptions could not be bettered today. We know against what Johnson was defending himself by his obsessional rituals, and what kind of thoughts he was attempting to expel. Johnson was subject to recurrent depression; to what he called 'a vile melancholy', and was plagued by constant guilt. Throughout most of his life he feared insanity. He hated going to bed because, once alone, morbid thoughts were sure to plague him, as Joshua Reynolds had observed. He was preoccupied with death and said that he never experienced a moment in which death was not terrible to him. He condemned himself for indolence, for having sensual thoughts, for indulgence in food and drink. This marvellous writer and lexicographer, who accomplished so much, wrote of himself, 'I have lived totally useless.'[11]

Johnson is a fascinating and sad example of a man who

kept depression at bay with obsessional defences during most of his life, but whose defences failed at times so that he was precipitated into a slough of despond. It is interesting that Johnson prescribed intellectual activity for a fellow-sufferer who was plagued with guilt. He himself turned to arithmetical calculations in order to divert himself; an early example of what behaviour therapists might call 'thought stopping'.

In severe cases of obsessive-compulsive disorder, the commonest ritual is compulsive washing. Patients may spend three or more hours in the bath or shower every morning, take two further hours to dress, and then feel compelled to have another bath each time they use the lavatory. There are many other types of ritual. I once knew a woman who was so concerned about the length of her skirt that it took her many hours to dress, and many visits to the dressmaker to demand alterations. If her skirt was too long, people would despise her for being frumpish: if too short, they would condemn her for being sexually provocative. Fear of contamination can become so severe that the patient may, paradoxically, come to lie in bed all day in a condition of squalor. Howard Hughes, the American multi-millionaire, is a striking example. His preoccupation with infection by micro-organisms led to such extreme rituals that he ended up wearing nothing but a pair of underpants and became incapable of looking after himself.

Severe ritual compulsions become so dissociated from the rest of the personality that they take on a life of their own. Sufferers complain that they know that their behaviour is ridiculous, but that they 'cannot help it'. In a recent book, Dr Judith Rapoport makes the illuminating suggestion that some obsessional rituals can be conceived as patterns of behaviour which were originally adaptive, but which have become dissociated and therefore exaggerated. As she points out, there is a parallel between some encoded forms of animal behaviour and obsessive-compulsive rituals. 'Cleaning, avoiding, checking, and repeating relate to the most basic preoccupations of cleanliness, safety, aggression, and sex. When they are carried out of context, they make no sense. The most convincing evidence will come when we find key "releasers" of these behaviors, analogous to the hormones that typically set off such patterns in animals.'[12] Rituals which are dissociated to this extent have to be brought under control by methods other than psychotherapy.

There are two reasons for thinking that obsessive-compulsive rituals of this severity are in a different diagnostic category from the mildly compulsive behaviour described above in connection with 'normal obsessional' personalities. The first is that the personalities of those who develop severe obsessive-compulsive illness are what I have described as 'normal obsessional' in only about 20% of cases. In other words, the illness can seldom be regarded as merely an exaggeration of the sufferer's habitual behaviour. Moreover, although the patients with severe obsessive-compulsive illness may be fanatic about their particular obsessions, they are quite often easy-going or even slovenly in other respects. This is quite different from 'normal obsessionals', whose meticulousness usually shows itself in every aspect of their behaviour. About 50% of these severe forms of illness originate in childhood. At the time of onset, boys are more subject to these disorders than girls; but, by the time adulthood is reached the incidence is about the same in each sex.

Secondly, severe obsessive-compulsive rituals occur in a variety of brain diseases, and are, in some instances, responsive to drugs which alter brain chemistry. Obsessive-compulsive symptoms have been described following the development of epilepsy; after head injury; as part of post-encephalitic Parkinsonism; and, as already mentioned, in patients suffering from Gilles de la Tourette's syndrome.

Whilst some forms of ritual can be brought under control by different techniques of behaviour therapy, recent work suggests that treatment by clomipramine hydrochloride (Anafranil) may be effective in some patients. But, although good results have been obtained in some very severe cases, others are unaffected, and further research is needed to elucidate which cases are most likely to respond to which variety of treatment.

References
1. Freud, Sigmund (1908) *Character and Anal Erotism*, Standard Edition, Collected Works, Vol. 9, p. 169, London: Hogarth Press and Institute of Psycho-Analysis (1959).
2. Ibid., pp. 172–3.
3. Parker, Dorothy, (1958) *Writers at Work*. The Paris Review Interviews. Vol. I, p. 72. London: Secker and Warburg.
4. Storr, Anthony (1972) *The Dynamics of Creation*, Chapter 8. London: Secker and Warburg.
5. Freud, Sigmund (1913) *The Disposition to Obsessional Neurosis*, Standard Edition, Collected Works, Vol. 12, p. 325. London: Hogarth Press and Institute of Psycho-Analysis (1958).
6. Brain, Russell (1960), *Some Reflections on Genius*, pp. 69–100. London, Pitman Medical Publishing.
7. Bate, Walter Jackson (1984) *Samuel Johnson*, p. 125, pp. 382–3, London: Hogarth Press.
8. Boswell, James (1799) *The Life of Samuel Johnson, LL.D.*, ed. Birkbeck Hill. Vol. I, pp. 484–5. Oxford: The Clarendon Press (1887).
9. Ibid., pp. 144–5.
10. Quoted in Brain, Russell (1960), p. 74.
11. Boswell, James (1799) Vol. I, p. 482, (1887).
12. Rapoport, Judith L. (1989) *The Boy who Couldn't Stop Washing*, p. 199, New York: E. P. Dutton.

12

The Schizoid Personality

The people we have designated as hysterical and depressive personalities are predominantly extraverted, and share an obvious concern with their relationships with other people. Hysterics seem principally concerned with obtaining attention, whilst depressives are more preoccupied with gaining approval. Both kinds of person have difficulty in managing aggressive impulses towards others. Hysterics tend to criticise the objects of their affections for not living up to their imagined ideals; whilst depressives turn their criticisms against themselves. Both are dependent, and fear being abandoned by those upon whom their happiness seems to depend, and therefore spend most of their time in psychotherapy discussing their interpersonal relationships.

Obsessional personalities, on the whole, are more independent. As we have seen, their attitudes constitute defences against the emergence of hostility in interpersonal relationships, and they therefore tend either to placate others, or else to tyrannise them in the same way that they exert tyrannical control over themselves. These attitudes tend to keep others rather more at a distance; and it is characteristic of obsessionals to spend more time discussing their work and other relatively impersonal topics than do hysterics or depressives. Some obsessionals are more concerned with controlling their own hostility, and thus may be said to be closer to the depressive end of the scale: whilst others are more perturbed by the supposed hostility of other people, and are thus closer to becoming paranoid. However, obsessionals do behave as if hostility on either side was generally controllable; and thus are able to maintain their relations with other people, albeit in what is often a rather rigid and formalised manner.

There is, however, a more deeply disturbed type of person whose fear of involvement with others is so extreme that he withdraws into himself and attempts to do without human relationships as far as possible. These are the people we call schizoid. Schizoid people come to the attention of psychotherapists in a variety of ways. Because they have little faith in the ability of others to understand or help them, they are often pressed into seeking help by those who are near enough to them to realise that there is something wrong. Thus, to take a characteristic example, an undergraduate who is failing at his work and who shows no signs of being able to make friends or enjoy university life may be steered into psychotherapy by a tutor. This will constitute an additional difficulty in therapy, though not necessarily an insurmountable one. If self-referred, such a patient will complain of not being able to make relation-ships, especially with the opposite sex; or of being quite unable to concentrate on work or complete work; or of what he is likely to call depression.

Although schizoid patients do indeed become depressed, their mood is often more of apathy than melancholia. As Fair-bairn has aptly observed, the 'characteristic affect of the schizoid state is undoubtedly a sense of futility'.[1] Although schizoid people may at first sight resemble depressed patients, one quickly comes to realise that their kind of depression has a quality of meaninglessness which is not present in the ordinary case of depression. Depressives, one feels, are suffering from an interruption or bad episode in their lives; and their resentment can be felt to be just below the surface. With schizoid people, one feels that their mood of futility is much more integral to their ordinary adaptation; almost as if their lives never had had much meaning.

Schizoid people are often difficult to interview. The therapist feels that he is 'not on the same wave-length'. When trying to take a history, he is likely to feel that, although the patient may be superficially co-operative in answering questions, he doesn't really 'give' anything. The patient may induce in the interviewer the feeling that, in answer to every query, he is really wanting to say: 'what on earth is the point of asking me that?' Some schizoid patients appear to affect an air of superiority, especially if, as is not infrequent, they are intellectually superior, and have made their chief adaptation to the world by means of their brains rather than their feelings. It is important not to allow oneself to be put off by this. Therapists like to have their efforts appreciated, and it is disconcerting to be faced with an individual who appears to repudiate every attempt to get to know and understand him.

It is important to realise that patients of this kind are deeply frightened of any kind of intimacy. Their defence is to withdraw as far as possible from emotional involvement. But since it is emotional involvement which gives meaning to life, they are constantly threatened with finding life meaningless. If the therapist is sufficiently mature to tolerate being repudiated and made to feel useless by such patients, he will find them of great interest, and, if he manages to penetrate their defences, will find himself richly rewarded by winning the trust of someone who for years has found it difficult to trust any other human being.

Why are persons of this kind so reluctant to allow anyone to become close to them? There seem to me to be three main types of fear of intimacy. All three may be present together; but one type is often more manifest than the others. First, a person may be reluctant to embark upon a relationship because he fears that it will end, and that he will therefore be worse off than if he had never taken the risk of involvement. This fear is often based upon an actual experience of loss in early childhood. Isaac Newton, for example, showed many schizoid traits of character. He was notably isolated, and never made any close emotional relationships with anyone of either sex. He was also extremely suspicious, reluctant to publish his work, and prone to accuse others of having stolen his discoveries. When he was just over fifty, he had a psychotic breakdown in which paranoid ideas were prominent. At least some of his emotional difficulties may reasonably be assumed to have taken origin from the experience of his early childhood. Newton was a premature child whose father had died before he was born. For the first three years of his life, he enjoyed the undivided attention of his mother. Then, when he was just past his third birthday, his mother remarried. She not only presented Newton with an unwanted stepfather, but added insult to injury by abandoning him, leaving him to be brought up by his maternal grandmother whilst she herself moved to live in a different house with her new husband. We know from his own writings that Newton felt this to be a betrayal. He seems never entirely to have trusted any human being again.[2]

A second reason for avoiding intimacy is the fear of being dominated and overborne by the other person to the point of losing identity as a separate individual. We all begin life being at the mercy of adults who are much more powerful that we are, and we all strive, in varying ways, to reach a degree of independence. Although some people wish to continue to be subject to the authority of others, and to have many of the decisions of life made for them, even the most masochistic prefer to retain some autonomy. This can be detected in very small children, and many children's games are concerned with demonstrating that they can put down adults and be 'king of the castle'. As children grow up, most learn that they can make their voices heard, and exercise some power over events, even whilst they are with people who are more powerful than themselves. They discover that, although they may not be able entirely to have their own way, they can exert influence and make others take notice of their wants and opinions. The people we call schizoid, on the contrary, conceive that they can only retain autonomy if they withdraw into isolation. They do not imagine that they can exert any influence over the thoughts or behaviour of others, whom they think of as being both more powerful and more ruthless than themselves. They think of other people as being so entirely oblivious of their needs and wishes that they might as well not exist, and so come to feel that their very being is threatened. R. D. Laing gives a good example of this in his book *The Divided Self*. One patient is arguing with another in the course of a session in an analytic group. One breaks off to say: 'I can't go on. You are arguing in order to have the pleasure of triumphing over me. At best you win an argument. At worst you lose an argument. I am arguing in order to preserve my existence.'[3]

Although at first sight such a statement might seem delusional, there may be more in it literally than meets the eye. Bruno Bettleheim,[4] the psychoanalyst who was for a year confined in Dachau and Buchenwald concentration camps, observed that those prisoners who surrendered autonomy entirely and acquiesced in letting the guards determine their whole existence became like automata – Mussulmen, as they were called – and soon actually died. Survival seemed to depend upon preserving some tiny area in which decision could still be in the hands of the prisoner himself.

The fear of being overborne or engulfed, as Laing calls it, sometimes seems to be the consequence of having been treated with particular lack of consideration as a child; more particularly, of having been treated as a doll or automaton or as an appendage to the parents rather than as a person with a separate existence. The fear has much in common with Freud's 'castration anxiety', in the sense of being deprived of potency or effectiveness.

The impotence of being unable to influence authority has been vividly depicted by the novelist Kafka in his classic novels *The Trial* and *The Castle*.[5,6] According to Kafka's biographer, Max Brod, Kafka continued, throughout his life, to attribute almost magical powers to his father.[7] When he was 36 he wrote a long *Letter to my Father* in which he exposed his continuing sense of inadequacy and his feeling of always being in the wrong which he experienced in relation to his father. The same sense of powerlessness is evident in Kafka's religious attitude. There is an Absolute, but so remote from the life of man that misunderstanding and lack of comprehension is inevitable. Kafka considered that parents were tyrants and slave-drivers. He agreed with Swift that 'parents are the least of all to be trusted with the education of their children'. His novels are concerned with authorities who are so arbitrary and unpredictable that it was impossible to understand them or work out ways of dealing with them.

I wrote earlier that neurotic symptoms were exaggerations of anxieties we all feel. Those who are fortunate enough to possess basic trust in other human beings may find it difficult to empathise with schizoid people because they cannot detect any trace of similar traits in their own personalities. However, even the most 'normal' people fear revealing intimate secrets to others; for they realise that to do so is to put oneself in the power of the other person. Real intimacy is not lightly embarked on even by those who are not habitually suspicious. The common fear of getting married is often rooted in the idea that to do so might threaten autonomy to a dangerous extent. Many people who pass for normal are unable to conceive of a human relationship in which the partners are on equal terms, in which giving and taking are reciprocal, because they have never experienced such a relationship, and may feel that they themselves have nothing much to give.

A third reason for avoiding intimacy is the subject's fear that he will harm or destroy the person to whom he becomes attached. At first sight this kind of fear may seem to contradict the other varieties since it seems to imply that the subject is more, not less, powerful than the other person. However, the power concerned is of a kind possessed by every child; the power to exhaust or empty the parent. Kleinian analysts would trace such a fear to phantasies arising in the earliest months of life, when a frustrated or greedy infant might suppose that his urgent need had emptied or destroyed the breast upon which his existence depended. However this may be, there is little doubt that older children may come to feel that their capacity to exhaust a parent outweighs the pleasure which the parent may take in their presence, especially if the parent is elderly or ailing. Schizoid adults habitually find that relations with others exhaust them, and so suppose that they themselves must be equally exhausting. This leads to a kind of careful watchfulness which makes spontaneity in human relationships impossible. In some instances, this attitude can be traced to the behaviour of a parent who is also schizoid. Small children are to some extent exhausting to most parents in our culture because their care requires constant vigilance and because they cannot provide the kind of interchange on equal terms which adults find rewarding. However, there are many parents who feel all too easily drained by their children because they themselves cannot play or enter into a child's world through their imagination. A child may thus be faced with a parent who not only does not give him the affection and understanding which he desperately needs, but who also conveys to him that his needs are potentially destructive of the person to whom he turns to fulfill them. This may lead to the conviction that fulfilment through love is unattainable except in phantasy. Close relationships are regarded as mutually exhausting rather than mutually rewarding; and so the safest thing is to avoid them as far as possible.

As we have seen, hysterical and depressive patients are generally anxious to please and therefore tend to make an agreeable first impression upon the therapist. Obsessional patients may be more reserved; but their fear of aggression usually makes them polite and respectful of convention. Some schizoid patients, on the other hand, often make little attempt to please, and may proclaim their disdain for convention by eccentricity in dress, disregard for good manners, and what may often seem to be deliberate lack of response to the utterances of the psychotherapist. Others appear to conform, and may, like obsessional patients, seem exceedingly polite and concerned with formality. Schizoid personalities who seem well adapted to reality sometimes present an impeccable 'persona' which may make their acquaintances, guests, and psychotherapists feel uncomfortable at their own lack of social polish. However, when people of this kind are faced with emotional demands, a child in trouble, or a wife who is depressed, their only recourse is to retreat from involvement. The emotions of others are as threatening as their own unacknowledged feelings, so that, instead of trying to understand or empathise with the person in distress, they shy away and recommend their own prescription, the only one known to them, redoubled self-control. It is only if the therapist understands what lies behind the mask of indifference or superiority which the schizoid patient assumes, and is prepared to control his own resentment at being disregarded or treated cavalierly, that he will be able to penetrate his patient's façade. Most of us maintain our self-esteem because we have fruitful, reinforcing relationships with others which make us feel valued. Although, as we have seen, depressive people are unusually dependent upon outside reinforcement to maintain self-esteem, all of us need this to some degree, and become depressed if we are isolated for any length of time. This was long ago recognised by the Russians who, when they arrest a political prisoner, customarily confine him alone without giving him any information about what is to be done with him or any news of his family and friends. After about six weeks of emotional isolation in which the prisoner's only exchanges are with gaolers who are forbidden to converse with him except about essentials, most prisoners become profoundly, hopelessly, depressed, and give up trying to care for themselves. Schizoid people are probably better able to stand solitary confinement than normal people because their relationships with others have been so tenuous that to be deprived of them is no great loss. What schizoid persons do is to develop a world of phantasy to compensate for their lack of fulfilment in the real world. Since schizoid persons have failed to obtain love or to achieve relationships on equal terms with anyone else, their phantasy is one in which they themselves play a superior role. If one cannot be loved, one can at least be admired, envied, or regarded with awe. This pose of superiority compounds the difficulty which schizoid people have in making relationships; for others detect it, and, quite naturally, resent it. And thus what began as a phantasy of being disliked or despised tends to become a reality. Some schizoid people attain what may appear to be good relations with others by going to the opposite extreme of the disdain for convention described above. Such a person will be punctiliously polite and exaggeratedly considerate, but those who are the recipients of his attention will tend to feel that his consideration comes from the head and not the heart. In this they will be right. Schizoid people sometimes make quite conscious decisions that it is morally right to be tactful, or generous, or virtuous; and strive to behave in accordance with their adopted principles. However, they will still convey to others their unconscious intention of keeping them at arm's length and fail to meet them on the common ground of shared humanity. St Paul's best known passage on love, from the first epistle to the Corinthians, is directly applicable to schizoid people.

'I may speak in tongues of men or of angels, but if I am without love, I am a sounding gong or a clanging cymbal. I may have the gift of prophecy, and know every hidden truth; I may have faith strong enough to move mountains; but if I have no love I am nothing. I may dole out all I possess, or even give my body to be burnt, but if I have no love, I am none the better.'[8]

Schizoid people, especially if intellectually gifted, may substitute power for love in actuality or phantasy, but the satisfaction which they obtain from this is both limited and precarious, for it seems that it is only the feeling of loving and being loved which is finally effective in dispelling a sense of futility.

In the chapter on obsessional people, I said that they tended to relate to others in terms of domination versus submission, or superiority versus inferiority. This is true to an even greater extent of the schizoid person, although, because of his greater withdrawal from involvement, phantasy plays a more significant part in his relations. Thus, one often discovers that a schizoid person cherishes the notion that he is unusually gifted, or has some special insight into reality (both suppositions may be true), whilst at the same time being terrified of finding himself in the hands of others as if he was powerless to influence or affect them. Phobias of operations, of the dentist, or even of the hairdresser are not uncommon in schizoid patients who conceive that if they go so far as to let anyone do anything to them, they will be in danger of being totally destroyed. Such ideas are delusions in embryo. In understanding the schizoid patient, it is helpful to bear in mind the delusional systems of paranoid schizophrenics. Every psychiatrist is familiar with the patient who believes himself to be extremely important; royalty, or a great inventor, or some other kind of misunderstood genius, but who believes that his true worth is not recognised, and his position taken from him by the machinations of the Catholics or the Freemasons, or some other group of wicked persecutors. Schizoid people, in contrast with schizophrenics, retain sufficient grasp of reality to distinguish at least part of their phantasy life from reality and therefore retain their sanity. Instead of exhibiting frank delusions, they may be touchy, suspicious or litigious. Very often, they refuse to put their phantasied superiority to the test. Some schizoid people who, in youth, were brilliant passers of examinations, fail to live up to their early promise because they dare not expose what they have to offer to the light of criticism, as if they knew that a large element of phantasy entered into their own self-estimate.

Since relationships are conceived of in terms of superiority versus inferiority, the sexual phantasies of schizoid people are often sadomasochistic. Unable to conceive of being loved, they can imagine being admired for their strength, or think of themselves as dominating a partner who might otherwise disregard them. Sadomasochistic phantasies are certainly not confined to schizoid people, as their widespread occurrence in pornography demonstrates; though perhaps it might be closer to the truth to say that such literature appeals to a schizoid aspect of human nature which is ubiquitous. But schizoid people cannot imagine any other kind of sexual relationship since their imagination is confined to the childhood situation in which discrepancy of power between child and adult is an inescapable feature. Schizoid women, who are far less commonly encountered than schizoid men, conceive of themselves in a masochistic way, as objects upon whom the man can exercise his strength. Since schizoid people live so much in phantasy, whilst finding it difficult to make actual relationships with real people, they often make use of phantasy during sexual relations. Laing describes a man who could only have intercourse with his wife if he was imagining having intercourse with her. Others make use of phantasies which belong to a childhood phase of development before the child had discovered what sexual intercourse was actually like. Fetishistic and other phantasies of a deviant kind belong to this category. It will be recalled that Freud thought of fetishism in terms of a splitting of the ego, in which one part denied reality, whilst the other continued to accept reality at least in part. The difficulty which schizoid people encounter in establishing ordinary sexual relations may also be described in terms of their alienation from the body, both the bodies of others and their own bodies.

In the last chapter, reference was made to the tendency of obsessional patients toward 'intellectualisation'. Schizoid patients exhibit this tendency to an even greater degree. They exalt the mental at the expense of the physical to the point at which they identify themselves with their minds and are apt to regard their bodies as mere appendages with needs and desires which are often regarded as a nuisance; alien demands which interfere with the true reality, the life of the mind. Proust, who showed a number of schizoid traits, wrote: 'Indeed it is the possession of a body that is the great danger to the mind, to our human and thinking life . . .'[9] Freud defined the ego in terms of the body.[10] 'The ego is first and foremost a body ego, i.e. the ego is ultimately derived from bodily sensations, chiefly from those springing from the surface of the body.' Schizoid patients, perhaps because of some very early failure in relation with the mother, become 'out of touch' with the body, and, as we have seen, regard being closely 'in touch' with another person as potentially threatening. It is touch which gives most of us our sense of reality, as well as conveying closeness to another person. Although we regard being out of touch with the body as a symptom of disorder when we see it in our patients, it must not be forgotten that man's greatest intellectual achievements depend upon the possibility of disassociating oneself, at least temporarily, from the world of the body. As I demonstrated in *The Dynamics of Creation*,[11] a schizoid personality is probably obligatory for certain kinds of creative achievement. Those who have achieved most in the fields of abstract thought have mostly been solitary people, disinclined to, or incapable of, making close relationships with other human beings. Descartes, for example, refers to the body as possibly illusory, and distrusted the evidence of the senses. It is significant that the first principle of his philosophy, 'I think, therefore I am', makes mind more certain than matter, and, as Bertrand Russell pointed out, 'my mind (for me) more certain than the minds of others'.[12] Although schizoid personalities suffer from their isolation and may, to psychiatric eyes, appear pathological, it must be remembered that detachment from the subjective, which is obligatory for the pursuit of science, is a human capacity of vital significance for our whole adaptation. Scientists confine their objectivity to the laboratory, and are as humanly subjective as anyone else where personal relationships are concerned; but their capacity for detachment could reasonably be described as 'schizoid' although their total personalities are not necessarily of this type. Scientists who behaved 'objectively' to their wives, as if the latter were subjects for experiment rather than persons with whom to relate, would be exhibiting schizoid behaviour.

According to some authorities, regarding the demands of the body as alien to the self belongs to a very early stage of infantile development. Winnicott, for example, writes: 'In the area I am examining the instincts are not yet clearly defined as internal to the infant. The instincts can be as much external as can a clap of thunder or a hit. The infant's ego is building up strength and in consequence is getting toward a stage in which id-demands will be felt as part of the self, and not as environmental . . .'[13]

I am not primarily concerned with the possible causes of particular types of distorted character formation, since, as I indicated in an earlier passage, the various theories put forward to account for these distortions are impossible, in our present state of knowledge, to prove or disprove. They therefore remain articles of faith which are the source of disputes between the various psychotherapeutic 'schools'. However, I think most psychotherapists who have undertaken the treatment of schizoid patients would agree that it appears that something must have gone wrong between mother and baby at a very early stage of the schizoid patient's development. It is now possible to predict which parents are likely to be successful as parents and which unsuccessful by careful observation of the behaviour and attitudes of mothers during the prenatal period, the time of delivery of the baby, and some weeks after delivery.[14] No doubt many other factors enter into the production of schizoid individuals, including genetics, intelligence level, and experience in later childhood; but I guess that the earliest experience with the mother may turn out to be crucial, since many schizoid patients give a history of having found interaction with others difficult from the moment that they first encountered other children. The Kempes' research was carried out to see if, by conducting careful observations of maternal behaviour before and after the birth of the infant, it would be possible to predict which children would be at risk of physical injury. Their success in predicting which families would show abnormal patterns of parental behaviour is considerable; and I suggest that their techniques could provide a way of proving whether the later development of schizoid traits of character is in fact related to abnormalities of interaction between mother and infant.

Whatever the ultimate cause turns out to be, schizoid individuals develop a mask, or 'persona' as Jung called it, which conceals their feelings both from themselves and from others. It is as if their most basic, primitive, physical needs had somehow been repudiated at a crucial time in their development, with the consequence that they had adopted a pose and a manner of relating which pretended that these basic needs were unimportant. This way of looking at schizoid individuals is closely related to Winnicott's concept of the False Self versus the True

Self. Civilised life demands that we all develop a persona. Indeed, social life would be impossible if we were unable to be polite, show consideration when we ourselves may be tired or out of temper, or sometimes defer to the opinions of others more than we would like for fear of provoking embarrassingly vehement dissent. But with our intimates, and especially with our partners in love, we ought to be able to shed the mask and risk being our vulnerable, emotional selves without constraint. This the schizoid person cannot do. He is terrified that his True Self will be rejected, repudiated, or even annihilated. Over many years he has built up a False Self, based upon compliant identification with others, until he himself finds it hard to recognise what his own deepest feelings really are. This may enable him to get by for many years, with no-one recognising that there is much wrong, although people may complain that he is difficult to know, or that he does not reveal much of himself. Psychiatrists long ago noticed that schizophrenic patients often were described as unusually good, well-behaved children. This compliance with the demands of parents sometimes indicates that a child's true individuality, his 'True Self' is already buried; and the outbreak of psychosis may, as R. D. Laing has emphasised, be an attempt of the True Self to emerge into the light of day. (There are many objections to regarding all cases of schizophrenia in this light, as Laing tends to do; but this way of looking at some 'schizophrenic episodes' in adolescence is fruitful.) Winnicott describes one patient who came to him after having a considerable amount of analysis with other analysts. 'My work really started with him when I made it clear to him that I recognised his non-existence. He made the remark that over the years all the good work done with him had been futile because it had been done on the basis that he existed, whereas he had only existed falsely. When I said that I recognised his non-existence he felt that he had been communicated with for the first time. What he meant was that his True Self that had been hidden away from infancy had now been in communication with his analyst in the only way which was not dangerous.'[15]

Schizoid individuals often feel most real when they are alone. Then their true selves can be allowed to flourish without danger of harm from others. If they happen to be gifted in one of the arts or sciences, they may find that creative activity is an effective compensation for their lack of close or genuine relationships with other people, and thus avoid suffering from a sense that life is futile or meaningless. As Winnicott observes: 'It is creative apperception more than anything else that makes the individual feel that life is worth living. Contrasted with this is a relationship to external reality which is one of compliance, the world and its details being recognised but only as something to be fitted in with or demanding adaptation. Compliance carries with it a sense of futility for the individual and is associated with the idea that nothing matters and that life is not worth living.'[16] By 'creative apperception' Winnicott means a whole attitude to life; one in which the individual feels that he is able to bring his whole personality into relation with other people and the world. Creative people vary very considerably in personality, as I have shown in *The Dynamics of Creation*.[17] By no means all are predominantly schizoid, and their work need not primarily represent a retreat from real life. But, provided they have the necessary talent, creative work does have a special appeal to those of schizoid temperament because its solitary practice means that they can pursue their own thoughts and phantasies without encountering the withering, shrivelling effect of others' scrutiny. If they then publish a book, or exhibit a picture, they will of course be sensitive to its reception; since it is bound to reveal something of their inner life, their 'True Self' But the work in which they are thus revealed will display only selected aspects, never the whole person. Moreover, it will have been prepared and polished in such a way as to make it as acceptable as possible. Many creative people feel so sensitive about 'work in progress' that they will not discuss it with anyone else or show it to anyone until it is entirely finished. What is spontaneously produced, before their own critical scrutiny has been brought to bear upon it, cannot be displayed; and this avoidance of spontaneity is a notable feature of the schizoid person's whole adaptation. Some creative people, like Newton, keep their discoveries or their works to themselves; or may profess themselves incapable of finishing them. Newton feared that others would steal his discoveries. Those who cannot complete a book are generally protecting themselves against criticism. Still others, as Fairbairn points out, pretend that their works, once completed, are no longer of any importance to them. Fairbairn quotes the case of an artist who 'lost all interest in his pictures once they had been painted; and the completed pictures were characteristically either just dumped in the corner of the studio or treated simply as commodities for sale'.[18]

However, the majority of schizoid patients who come the way of the psychotherapist are not creative except in phantasy. The therapist's task is first to recognise the patient's isolation and then so to gain the patient's confidence that the defences which maintain his isolation need not continue. Often, the therapist will find it necessary to make a relationship with the patient in what may seem rather an intellectual fashion to begin with. Schizoid patients are easily frightened by a direct approach to their emotional life. Educated patients of this type will often reveal an interest in literature or the other arts, since these afford an opportunity for emotional expression which does not involve other people. I have found it valuable to explore with such patients what books or music or painting particularly appeal to them. This exploration can lead to a feeling of shared emotional experience which may form a basis upon which the patient feels safe to proceed further. It is important that the therapist is not prematurely discouraged because the patient does not show any immediate response. Progress with these deeply disturbed people is bound to be slow; but, very often, a great deal more is happening during the course of psychotherapy than the patient at first acknowledges or even realises. If, for many years, one's adaptation has been in the direction of doing without other people as far as possible, it is not likely that one will admit a need for them very easily. The most difficult thing for the schizoid patient to give up is his phantasied superiority. Indeed, he may never quite be able to relinquish this, since his whole self-esteem has for years depended upon it. We see this even more clearly in the case of patients who are frankly psychotic. The delusions of the schizophrenic cannot be argued with, because their maintenance has become essential to the patient's conception of himself as a person. If one's only source of self-esteem is the belief that wicked persecutors have deprived one of one's birthright, that belief will not be susceptible to argument. It is only when the schizoid person comes to believe that other people really care for him that he can afford to abandon his phantasy of superiority: that is, when he has been able to discover that love is a better source of self-esteem than power.

Whereas the delusions of the schizophrenic are private, that is, not shared by other people, which may be one reason why we label him mad, beliefs of an almost equally strange kind may be shared by small numbers of people whose psychopathology often seems to be schizoid. The reason for this is that esoteric beliefs and phantasied superiority go hand in hand. The alienated and the isolated are attracted to strange sects partly because the systems of belief which such sects promulgate hold out the promise of understanding their own difficulties in life, and partly because being a member of such a sect carries with it the implication of possessing more insight into life than the average person. It would be invidious to mention any particular sect, but I cannot forbear to say that, in my opinion, some groups of psychoanalysts comply with this description. There still exist analysts who believe that their particular variety of analysis is the only true key to human understanding; that there is such a thing as being completely, or fully, analysed; and that all those who do not pursue this particular path are consigned to outer darkness. It is analysts of this kind whom I had in mind when, in the chapter on interpretation, I referred to doctrinaire analysts who have not made adequate rapport with their patients and who only understand human nature in terms of a rigid doctrinal scheme.

Schizoid patients present the greatest challenge to the psychotherapist, unless he is one of those bold spirits who works with the frankly psychotic. But, to my mind, they are the most interesting of all the troubled people who consult us, and also those who teach us most about the complexities of human nature.

References
1. Fairbairn, W. Ronald D. (1976) *Psychoanalytic Studies of the Personality*, p. 51. London: Routledge and Kegan Paul.

2. Storr, Anthony (1972) *The Dynamics of Creation*, Chapter 6. London: Secker and Warburg.
3. Laing, R. D. (1960) *The Divided Self*, p. 45. London: Tavistock.
4. Bettleheim, Bruno (1961) *The Informed Heart*. London: Thames and Hudson.
5. Kafka, Franz (1925) *The Trial*, trans. Willa and Edwin Muir. London: Secker and Warburg.
6. Kafka, Franz (1930) *The Castle*, trans. Willa and Edwin Muir. London: Secker and Warburg.
7. Brod, Max (1948) *Franz Kafka: A Biography*. London: Secker and Warburg.
8. *New English Bible* (1970) p. 221. Oxford and Cambridge University Presses.
9. Proust, Marcel (1970) *Time Regained*, p. 456. Vol. XII of *Remembrance of Things Past*, trans. Andreas Mayor. London: Chatto and Windus.
10. Freud, Sigmund (1923) *The Ego and the Id*. Standard Edition, Collected Works, Vol. 19, p. 26 and footnote. London: Hogarth Press and Institute of Psycho-Analysis (1968).
11. Storr, Anthony (1972) *The Dynamics of Creation*, Chapters 5, 6. London: Secker and Warburg.
12. Russell, Bertrand (1955) *History of Western Philosophy*, p. 586. London: Allen and Unwin.
13. Winnicott, D. W. (1963) 'Ego Distortion in Terms of True and False Self', in *The Maturational Process and the Facilitating Environment*. London: Hogarth Press.
14. Kempe, Ruth S. and Henry, C. (1978) *Child Abuse*, p. 83. London: Fontana-Open Books.
15. Winnicott, D. W. (1963) ibid. p. 151.
16. Winnicott, D. W. (1971) *Playing and Reality*, p. 65. New York: Basic Books.
17. Storr, Anthony (1972) ibid.
18. Fairbairn, W. Ronald D. (1976) ibid. p. 19.

13

Cure, Termination
and Results

In medical practice, treatment is brought to an end either when
the patient is cured, or else when the doctor decides that as
much as can be done has been done to relieve a disability. In the
case of diseases like diabetes, asthma, or many forms of heart
disease, in which alleviation and control, rather than cure, are
the doctor's aim, treatment may be prolonged indefinitely.

In the practice of psychotherapy, some cases can be rapidly
and permanently cured; for example, certain varieties of impotence in men, or cases which centre around some painful or
shameful experience which haunts the patient, but which he
has been unable to face. I remember, for example, one case in
which a man was cured of his symptoms of anxiety in a single
psychotherapeutic session in which he revealed that he had left
his parents behind in Europe to the mercy of the Nazis, whilst
he himself took the opportunity to escape. His confession
brought considerable relief, and a follow-up some weeks later
revealed that he was free of symptoms.

In the early days of psychoanalysis, it was hoped that all
neurotic symptoms could be abolished in a reasonably simple
way, provided that their origin could be established and the
emotions connected with their origin recollected and worked
through. In *Studies on Hysteria*, the book which Freud wrote in
collaboration with Breuer, the authors write in their first paper:

'For we found, to our great surprise at first, that *each indi-*

146

vidual hysterical symptom immediately and permanently disappeared when we had succeeded in bringing clearly to light the memory of the event by which it was provoked and in arousing its accompanying affect, and when the patient had described that event in the greatest possible detail and had put the affect into words.[1]

Later, the same type of explanation was applied to obsessional symptoms. In the next volume of the Standard Edition, we read of a girl 'who had become almost completely isolated on account of an obsessional fear of incontinence of urine. She could no longer leave her room or receive visitors without having urinated a number of times. When she was at home or entirely alone the fear did not trouble her. *Reinstatement:* it was an obsession based on temptation or mistrust. She did not mistrust her bladder but her resistance to erotic impulses. The origin of the obsession shows this clearly. Once, at the theatre, on seeing a man who attracted her, she had felt an erotic desire, accompanied (as spontaneous pollutions in women always are) by a desire to urinate. She was obliged to leave the theatre, and from that moment on she was a prey to the fear of having the same sensation, but the desire to urinate had replaced the erotic one. She was completely cured.'[2]

If all neurotic symptoms were as clear-cut as this, and if their origin could be as easily determined, psychotherapy would be simpler than it is, and cure more clearly definable. Although there is a good deal more about that particular young lady which we should like to know, and which we are not told, her symptom can reasonably be regarded in the light of an alien intruder which was banished by psychotherapy in rather the same way as the bacteria causing an infection can be banished by an antibiotic; and, in such cases, it is legitimate to speak of 'cure'. In this example, it is also unlikely that there was any doubt as to when to bring treatment to an end, or any difficulty encountered in doing so.

Although behaviour therapists regard neurotic symptoms as learned maladaptive habits rather than as the consequence of repressed emotions, their original attitude to such symptoms was not dissimilar. That is, they hoped that neurotic symptoms could all be regarded as extraneous to the patient's personality, and that it might be possible to abolish them by behavioural techniques without it proving necessary to understand the patient as a whole or to make a relationship with him.

Neither Freud's original hope nor that of the behaviour therapists has been sustained; and it is interesting to watch the latter treading the same path as the former, albeit from a different point of departure.

Freud soon discovered that neurotic symptoms were not always easily reducible to repressed emotions having a particular origin at a particular time. The majority of neurotic symptoms are intimately bound up with the patient's personality, attitude to life, and often with his relationships with those persons who are close to him; so that their personalities and the effect that they have upon the patient may also have to be considered. Another factor which may have contributed to less emphasis being laid upon particular symptoms, and more upon the whole personality, was Freud's change of technique from hypnosis to free association. If the patient is encouraged to take the lead, and to say everything which comes into his head without concealment or the exercise of choice, it is surely inevitable that he will not only talk about his symptoms, however important or troublesome these may be, but about his aspirations, goals, relationships with others, interests, hopes, fears, achievements, and disappointments; in short, about everything which constitutes him as an individual and distinguishes him as an unique person.

Moreover, as psychoanalysts began to take into treatment a wider variety of persons than the hysterics for whom Freud and Breuer originated the 'talking cure', they realised that many patients who presented themselves for psychoanalysis did so because of peculiarities of character rather than because of definable neurotic symptoms. It was partly because analysts began to treat such people that lengthy analyses became the rule. It is often forgotten that, in the early days of psychoanalysis, treatments were brief; sometimes shorter than many behaviour therapy programmes today. In his *New Introductory Lectures* Freud writes: 'The analysis of character disorders also calls for long periods of treatment; but it is often successful; and do you know of any other therapy with which such a task could even be approached?'[3]

Today, many of the patients who seek psychotherapy are not

suffering from any definable neurosis, but from generalised unhappiness, difficulties in interpersonal relationships, problems with work − in fact, they have 'problems in living', as Szasz calls them. With such people, what the psychotherapist is aiming at is not so much the abolition of particular symptoms, as changes in attitude toward others and life in general. These changes, I believe, are most likely to be brought about through the agency of the specialised, professional, yet intensely personal relationship which the skilled therapist makes with his patient; and this is why, throughout this book, my emphasis has been upon types of person rather than upon types of neurosis. The change which has come about in psychotherapy from a primary concern with symptoms to a primary concern with whole persons has had a number of consequences, some of which are still not fully appreciated by psychotherapists themselves. One, to which I shall return, is that, in spite of Freud's hope that he would make it so, psychotherapy cannot be a scientific enterprise. Although the psychotherapist needs to retain a measure of objectivity in relation to his patient, he must allow himself to be affected by the patient if he is to understand him. Since the therapist forms part of a reciprocal relationship, albeit of a specialised kind, he cannot maintain the kind of detachment which characterises the scientist conducting a chemical experiment. Understanding other people is, inescapably, a different enterprise from understanding things; and those who attempt to maintain towards people the kind of detached attitude which they might adopt toward things render themselves incapable of understanding others at all.

Another consequence of the change in psychotherapy is that 'cure', or even 'improvement', become much more difficult to assess. Freud's patient lost her phobia, and he had no hesitation in pronouncing her 'completely cured'. But the changes in attitude which lead to increased confidence, competence, and enjoyment are imponderables which, although some attempts can be made to assess them by means of the questionnaires beloved of psychologists, are much harder to measure.

Because, in most cases, the presenting symptoms which bring the patient to seek psychotherapy cannot be regarded as extraneous, but are closely connected with the patient's whole personality, they generally fade into insignificance once the psychotherapeutic process is under way. Psychotherapy began as one thing and has turned into something different without sufficient acknowledgement of the change by its practitioners. Although, during the course of psychotherapy, patients do lose symptoms, − for example, the tension induced by excessive anxiety, depression, a sense of futility, inability to concentrate or finish work, and a variety of difficulties in relationships with others − it seems to me that the loss of such symptoms, or the diminution in intensity which is, perhaps, a more common consequence of our efforts, is secondary to something more important which is a central feature of many different forms of psychotherapy, but which is not easy to define. In other words, improvement, or 'getting better', may be partially independent of, or unconnected with, the disappearance of symptoms. To illustrate what I mean, I will give an example from my own practice. Some time ago I had a letter from a man whom I had treated some twenty-five years previously asking whether I would see, or at any rate advise treatment for, his daughter. He assumed, wrongly, that I would not remember him, and, in the course of his letter, wrote as follows: 'I can quite truthfully say that six months of your patient listening to my woes made a most important contribution to my life style. Although my transvestism was not cured my approach to life and to other people was re-orientated and for that I am most grateful. It is part of my life that I have *never* forgotten.'

Looked at from one point of view, my treatment of this man was a failure. His major symptom, the complaint which drove him to seek my help, was not abolished. And yet I think it is clear that he did get something from his short period of psychotherapy which was of considerable value to him. A man does not write to a psychotherapist asking him to see his daughter, twenty-five years after his own treatment was over, using the terms employed in this letter, unless he believes that what happened during his period of treatment was important.

Today, such a patient might well be referred to a behaviour therapist. The attempt to abolish sexually perverse behaviour by associating such behaviour with noxious stimuli − aversion therapy − has not proved as effective as was originally hoped; but a behavioural programme designed to encourage an increase in normal sexual behaviour at the expense of the perversion might well have been helpful to some extent. If the patient's sexual relationship with his wife had improved, other benefits might have followed; for example, he might have felt himself to be more like, and more on equal terms with, other men. If the behavioural approach of concentrating on the symptom had been adopted, would this man have missed anything which he gained from psychotherapy?

This is not an easy question to answer; but I think that it is important to realise that transvestism is more than a learned maladaptive habit. It is extremely complex compulsion, in which distaste for, or fear of, sexual intercourse is one element; lack of confidence in masculinity and failure in masculine identification another; masochism often a third. This particular patient had a weak father and a mother who 'wore the trousers'. When he identified himself with his mother by dressing in female clothes he, paradoxically, felt more of a man. The fact that he came to understand some of the mechanisms at work in his compulsion did not abolish it; but it did at least make sense of it to him with the consequence that he no longer felt so ridiculous; and diminution in his sense of shame led to an increase in self-confidence and hence to better interpersonal relationships.

However, understanding the psychopathology of his symptoms was not the only consequence of his psychotherapy. In the letter from which I have quoted, the essential phrase is: 'My approach to life and to other people was re-orientated', and I find it hard to believe that this result could have been achieved in the absence of the kind of personal relationship which was achieved during the period of his psychotherapy.

In medical practice, different complaints require different treatments. Psychotherapists have often been criticised for offering neurotic patients the same treatment, whatever their initial complaint. Now that we are beginning to treat some kinds of neurotic symptom by behavioural and other methods, there is some justification for this criticism, though less than at first appears, since patients who seek, and respond to, psychotherapy have much in common, however they may differ in psychopathology.

First, they do not understand themselves; and, second, they do not accept certain parts of themselves. These two features may be aspects of the same phenomenon. For example, the over-compliant person who suffers from always being overborne by others does not understand that, at an early stage in his development he repressed the assertive, aggressive aspect of his personality; and finds it hard to accept that he has such an aspect to his personality. Although one may understand certain things in oneself and still deplore them, like greed or selfishness, it is nevertheless true that one cannot accept the things that one does *not* understand. One thing which certainly facilitates self-acceptance is acceptance by another person. It is difficult to change unless one both accepts and understands oneself, for how can one change anything if one is reluctant to admit its existence? A schizoid person, for example, may have to recognise that beneath his façade of superiority is a frightened child. How can he possibly begin to overcome his fears unless he recognises their existence? Moreover, he has to learn to deal with that frightened child within himself as he would, one hopes, deal with a frightened child whom he encountered in the external world. Many patients are much more harsh to the child within themselves than they would be to their own children, although some are harsh to both. Something can be achieved by bullying, but not very much; the child who is beaten for school refusal may continue to go to school for some time; but he is likely to become a truant or to develop some illness which will excuse his attendance unless his fears are investigated and understood.

Understanding another person in detail and in depth, which is required in psychotherapy, demands that the psychotherapist has knowledge of what is, unfortunately, called 'psychopathology'. I think this term should be dropped. It dates from the time when psychotherapists were consulted by people with obvious neurotic symptoms rather than 'problems in living', and I am not so sure that it was an appropriate term to use even in their case. For which of us has never had neurotic symptoms? Character itself is a matter of 'defences', another term which is inappropriate, since no human being could possibly manage his life without defences of various kinds. The kind of 'psychopathology' which I have tried to present in this book is primarily descriptive, rather than being concerned with causes. Although I myself believe that the atmosphere in which a child was reared does have a profound effect upon the development of his character, and although I have ventured to proffer partial explanations of adult character in terms of possible childhood influences, such explanations are not essential in understanding. For example, I postulated that the primary or most important feature of the people we call 'depressive' was an absence of built-in self-esteem; and I suggested that whether a person developed an adequate sense of self-esteem might depend upon how he felt his parents had regarded him in childhood. Suppose that this explanation is wrong. It nevertheless remains true that the adult depressive has very little self-esteem, and that this provides some kind of explanation of his vulnerability to reverses in life, whatever the origin of this deficiency may be. When Freud began the practice of psychoanalysis, he was, as I have already stated, concerned to trace the origin of particular symptoms; to discover their cause in some traumatic event occurring at an identifiable time. However appropriate this way of proceeding may be in the case of traumatic neurosis or certain kinds of hysterical symptom, it is not, in my view, important in understanding most of the difficulties with which patients seeking psychotherapy present us today. As I said when discussing obsessional patients, it does not matter whether or not a patient's tendency to be overconcerned with tidiness and cleanliness took origin from rigorous toilet-training or not. It does matter that the psychotherapist understands the anxieties against which meticulous tidiness and cleanliness are defences.

In understanding patients, it is necessary for the psychotherapist to understand the background from which a patient came, and how he developed during the course of his childhood. If one thinks of one's intimate friends, one generally knows a good deal about their background; where they were brought up, what sort of a family they came from, what kind of childhood they had. Indeed, I think one could hardly claim to know anyone intimately unless one did have some idea of these matters. But, understanding the course of a person's childhood is not the same as assuming that the whole of his adult personality was formed by the events of his childhood. What he himself picks out as significant events may be determined by the genetic substructure of his personality. As Rycroft pointed out in his paper 'Beyond the Reality Principle'[4] Freud was too much inclined to regard the infant as totally passive, and therefore completely at the mercy of the moulding power of external forces. But, as every mother knows, even new-born infants differ markedly, and the infant's adaptation to the reality of the mother is an active process to which both participants contribute.

Some patients certainly have appalling childhoods; and I am not suggesting that their adult difficulties are not related to their childhood experiences. But I am trying to make the point that what one child finds traumatic another may not. I am also trying to dispel the notion that psychotherapy is primarily a kind of treasure hunt for traumatic incidents. Although a few hysterical symptoms may immediately and permanently disappear when the therapist has, to repeat Freud's words, 'succeeded in bringing clearly to light the memory of the event by which it was provoked and in arousing its accompanying affect', the more generalised symptoms of unhappiness and difficulty in interpersonal relations which most of our patients bring to us do not improve in this way.

How do they improve? First, as I wrote when discussing transference, by means of the changing relationship with the therapist who, right from the very beginning of his encounter with the patient, must be alert to the patient's attitude toward himself. Is he frightened, in awe, envious, obsequious, seductive, contemptuous, dependent, or defensive? As the patient becomes aware, in the here-and-now, of what his attitude toward the therapist is, of how this attitude is relevant to his attitude toward the people in his life with whom he has difficulties, and of how his habitual attitudes toward others may have been appropriate or the only possible ones in childhood when they first began to manifest themselves, but have persisted inappropriately—as the patient begins to be aware of all this, so he begins to be able to alter his attitudes, first toward the therapist, and then toward others.

Second, he becomes aware of his own psychopathology, or psychology, as I should prefer to call it. Does insight, or understanding oneself better, actually have any influence upon happiness or difficulties in relating to others? Yes, in one way it does. I have already said that, as patients learn to accept themselves, many symptoms of the more general kind tend to disappear or at least to be alleviated. Acceptance by the therapist facilitates self-acceptance, and this relieves the misery of feeling unacceptable. But, let us face the fact that psychotherapy may not be able to alter basic character structure. I do not believe that there is any convincing evidence that even years of analysis, in the most expert hands, radically alters a person's fundamental 'psychopathology'. I think that analysts originally hoped that it could, and that some analysts still deceive themselves into thinking that it can. However, most will surely admit that a person's tendency toward depression, or his use of obsessional or schizoid types of defence will not be abolished, however much he learns to understand, control, and make use of these fundamental aspects of his personality. But I believe that it is still important for the patient to understand even those features of his personality which are not amenable to change. I take the view that neurosis is not so much a matter of possessing a particular type of psychopathology as of being overwhelmed by that psychopathology, or of being unable to make effective use of it. We all have the same varieties of psychopathology as do our patients, in varying degree. If we did not, we could not understand them. But we are not, at any rate for most of the time, overwhelmed by, or demoralised by, our psychopathology. It is sometimes forgotten that Freud wrote: 'The neuroses are, as we know, disorders of the ego.'[5] And Fenichel, who wrote that psychoanalytic bible *The Psychoanalytic Theory of Neurosis* states: 'All neurotic phenomena are based on insufficiencies of the normal control apparatus.'[6] I believe that much of the effect of successful psychotherapy depends upon the patient feeling that he is no longer at the mercy of what I must still continue to call his psychopathology, but able to experiment with his own nature and make creative use of it. The therapist, by understanding his patient, can act as a mirror, reflecting back to the patient aspects of himself which he had not seen or accepted. There is also a sense in which the therapist might be said to lend the patient his ego; or, as behaviour therapists might prefer to put it, provide a model for the patient to imitate. If one is faced with an unfamiliar task of which one is frightened, the fact that someone else seems to regard the same task as manageable helps one to tackle it. Patients come into therapy demoralised by the problems with which their own psychology confronts them. The fact that the therapist is familiar with such problems, understands them, and regards them as something which can be faced and dealt with, lends the patient the courage to approach them in the same way. The effect of suggestion can never be excluded from any kind of psychotherapy, nor should it be; but this kind of indirect suggestion, conveyed solely by the therapist's attitude of confidence, is a very different matter from its deliberate employment in the form of hypnosis and the like, which, by putting the patient in the position of a child, increases his sense of inadequacy.

This view of the nature of psychotherapy calls into question the whole concept of cure as originally put forward by the pioneer psychoanalysts, who believed that, by the undoing of defences, and the consequent emergence into consciousness of repressed material, all neurotic symptoms would be abolished and the patients could be restored to some state labelled 'normal'.

One of my teachers, Emanuel Miller, used to refer to the normal man as 'a very dark horse'. I would go even further and say that the normal man is not so much a dark horse as a mythical one.

Mythical also are those states of perfection labelled 'emotional maturity', 'integration', 'self-realisation', 'full genitality', or the achievement of 'mature object relationships'. All these terms refer to goals toward which we may legitimately strive, but at which we never arrive.

If we dispense with myth, can we attempt to define what improvement or 'getting better' in the course of, or as a result of, psychotherapy really is? Interestingly, there is quite a consensus of opinion between psychotherapists of very different approaches.

Jung, for example, used to say that analysis was for people who found themselves stuck; and his objective was to get them moving again. 'In the majority of my cases the resources of the conscious mind are exhausted (or, in ordinary English, they are "stuck"). . . . My aim is to bring about a psychic state in which my patient begins to experiment with his own nature – a state of fluidity, change and growth where nothing is eternally fixed and hopelessly petrified.'[7]

This is very similar to Carl Rogers' statement that 'Clients seem to move toward more openly being a process, a fluidity, a changing'. He quotes Kierkegaard as saying that 'An existing individual is constantly in process of becoming . . . and translates all his thinking into terms of process'.[8] As Kierkegaard realised, this description is characteristic of writers and other creative individuals, who show in their work that they are constantly developing and changing; never reaching a goal, but always stretching out toward something new. Creative individuals differ from other people in possessing particular skills, so that they demonstrate this process of becoming in their work; but it seems to me likely that this process of development and change takes place in all individuals who are not paralysed by neurosis or psychosis. Travelling hopefully toward the future, instead of being stuck in the stereotyped attitudes of childhood and the past, means to be able to modify and make use of one's psychopathology rather than getting rid of it. Another change which occurs as the result of successful psychotherapy is that the patient comes to feel increasing confidence in his own judgement. Thomas Szasz, the controversial American psychoanalyst, defines the aim of psychoanalytic treatment as being 'to increase the patient's knowledge of himself and others and hence his freedom of choice in the conduct of his life'.[9] Szasz is particularly insistent that the therapist should not give advice or do anything else which might interfere with the patient's autonomy; indeed, he calls his own brand of psychoanalysis 'autonomous psychotherapy'. Rogers also notes that the client who improves 'increasingly trusts and values the process which is himself'.[10] It is very characteristic of depressed and dependent people that they attribute more value to the judgement of others than to their own; which is why, during the course of therapy, the therapist must always take the attitude of helping the patient to find his own answers rather than guiding him or giving him direct advice. Part of growing up is to realise that one's own thoughts and feelings may be trustworthy guides for oneself, even if others do not necessarily find them so, for them.

In discussing schizoid people, I made reference to Winnicott's concept of the false self; an idea expanded by R. D. Laing. It is clear that being able to drop this particular form of defence is another way of changing for the better; and it is interesting to note that Carl Rogers expresses just the same idea when he refers to patients who improve as moving 'away from façades'.[11]

The psychoanalyst W. R. D. Fairbairn in an interesting paper refers to 'the maintenance of the patient's internal world as a closed system'[12] as being the greatest of all sources of resistance. That is, he emphasises the fact that patients seem very often to have given up hope of finding relationships with real people in the external world satisfying; and therefore hold on to phantasied relationships derived from childhood to which they attempt to make real people conform. He quotes a case analogous to Laing's case of the man who could only have intercourse with his wife by imagining having intercourse with his wife. This case was of a woman who could only bring herself to have intercourse with her husband if she immersed herself in phantasies which, Fairbairn says represented an infantile sexual relationship with her father. That is, she could not engage in the free give and take of actual relationships with a real person, but had to experience this in terms of preconceived notions derived from her early childhood. Fairbairn sees the analyst's task as penetrating the internal world of the patient and making it accessible to reality. Rogers is surely expressing a similar idea when he says that change is manifested by an increased ability to experience the world more nearly as it is instead of in terms of preconceived categories; an increased openness to experience.

I think all these formulations have in common the idea that change and development is part of human existence, and that when people feel that they are changing and developing they are living satisfactorily. Neurotic people, because of fears and anxieties, tend to hold on to the past, and not to develop and change as they should. This is quite a different conception from treating neurosis as a kind of disease having specific causes which, when disinterred, can be abolished. I find the analogy with creative people particularly illuminating. As I said elsewhere, I have had a number of creative people as patients. It was only when they got blocked, or stuck, that they needed me. When they were able to work, all was well.

The changes which occur as the result of successful psychotherapy do not lend themselves to precise description or measurement; and it is therefore difficult to suggest exact criteria for the termination of treatment. Most of the attempts to do so are unrealistically idealistic. However, one statement of the analyst's aim appeals to me as being closer to the truth of what actually happens in psychoanalytic psychotherapy than most. Annie Reich is quoted as saying that 'one should be content if one frees a patient from symptoms, and enables him to work, to adjust to reality, to engage in "adult object relations", and to accept his own limitations'.[13] I would modify this by saying that one may also have to be content if one fails to abolish symptoms completely, as in the case of the transvestist to which I have already referred. In practice, I have found that even inexperienced therapists come to recognise a point at which both therapist and patient conclude that as much as can be done has been done – at least at that particular point in the patient's life. In an ideal world, psychotherapy ought to go on for as long as is necessary for the patient to feel that he understands what kind of a person he is and what forces have helped to shape him; that he can face the ordinary challenges of life as competently as anyone else; and that he is capable of fulfilling relationships with other human beings on equal terms. In practice, psychotherapy has often to be limited in time, particularly within the National Health Service; since the demand exceeds the supply, and doctors often change their posts and move to another area, making it impossible to see any given patient for a very long period. However, it is certainly possible substantially to help a large number of patients who are seen once or twice per week over a period of a year or less, and there is some evidence to suggest that setting some kind of time limit may actually be beneficial. Moreover, patients who show improvement tend to do so during the early months of treatment; at least as regards the relief of symptoms. Jerome Frank found that most patients reported that improvement in their general sense of comfort occurred rapidly, and that relief of symptoms occurring during the first six months of treatment was usually permanent. He also found that the kind of improvement in interpersonal relationships which results in the patient becoming more socially effective was related to the amount of contact which the patient had with the therapist and therefore generally took longer.[14] It is clear that these findings are congruent with my earlier statement that psychotherapy had changed its primary concern from symptoms to persons as a whole. Another way of stating this would be to say than any analytical type of psychotherapy is now predominantly interested in improving a patient's interpersonal relationships through the agency of the transference; and that this is why analytical psychotherapy tends to be prolonged.

It follows from this that the patients who most need psychotherapy over a very long period – perhaps over many years – are those who have the most difficulty in interpersonal relationships. These are the patients I have described as schizoid. I would add to their number a few of the more seriously disturbed hysterics, whose disorder generally turns out to have a schizoid basis, as Fairbairn described. Anyone who is proposing to make psychotherapy a major part of his professional life ought to have experience in treating schizoid patients, since he will learn more from them than from any other kind of patient; but there is no point in avoiding the fact that such patients may require a very long period of contact with the therapist if the latter is to overcome their fears and suspicions and establish a relationship of trust. I have no easy answer to the objection that a National Health Service cannot be expected to provide adequate therapy for such people, except to say that the doctors who are sufficiently enthusiastic will not infrequently make considerable personal sacrifices of time to ensure that such patients do receive the help they need. Schizoid patients should not be referred to beginners. The suggestion that as much as can be done has been done may originate either with the patient or with the therapist. The first may say; 'I think I've got about as far as I can', and, if the therapist agrees, plans for termination can be made. In other cases, it may be the therapist who tentatively suggests that the end of therapy is in sight by saying something like, 'How would you feel about ending these sessions fairly soon?' When agreement has been reached, it is important that therapy is not too suddenly terminated. It must always be remembered that, if therapy has been at all successful, or, in some cases, even if what has been achieved seems very slight, the period of time during which the patient has been coming to see the therapist is likely to have been extremely important to him. As I have reiterated throughout this book, the psychotherapeutic situation is unique. Patients may look back upon it as the only time in their lives during which they feel themselves to have been understood and fully accepted by another human being. Even if they themselves do not demand it, it is only fair that termination of this important period should not be hurried. In most cases, a reduction in the frequency of visits to the therapist is advisable: from twice a week to once, and then to once a fortnight, once a month, and so on. In cases where the patient has been coming for two or more years, the period between deciding upon termination and putting it into effect may need to be as long as six months; in other cases, less. I have generally offered my patients a follow-up appointment six months after the termination of their therapy, partly in order to satisfy my own wish to know about their progress and welfare; and partly to reassure them that the relationship we have established is genuine, in spite of the limitations imposed by its professional nature. One would, I think, be quite inhuman if one did not wish to know how people one had got to know so intimately were faring.

Some patients are anxious to have done with therapy as soon as they possibly can; and these present no problem in termination other than that of deterring them from ending treatment prematurely. Such patients are not likely to keep follow-up appointments; possibly because they have found the position of being a patient humiliating, and do not wish to be reminded of it. Their reluctance to let the therapist know how they are progressing may also be related to what has been described as 'post-analytic improvement'. This phenomenon is particularly likely to occur in people who have been very dependent, but who find, to their own surprise, that, after psychotherapy, they can be much more independent than they had thought possible. For such people, re-involvement with the therapist, even if it is minimal, represents a threat to their new-found freedom. I have sometimes had letters from patients of this kind many years afterwards, apologising for not responding to my request to let me know how they were managing.

There are other patients who, if they could, would go on with therapy for ever. One skill which experienced therapists acquire is the ability to detect when a patient insists upon going on because of his dependency rather than because he needs to go on for other reasons; a skill more likely to be acquired when the therapist has no financial interest in his patient continuing to come and see him. During the course of therapy, dependency can usually be reduced by the therapist's refusal to give direct advice, and by his encouragement to the patient to seek his own answers to his problems. Careful weaning can usually be counted upon to deal with the problem of the dependent patient, and, as I wrote above, many patients are gratified by their discovery that, without the therapist, they are more competent than they had imagined that they could be. However, a small number of extremely insecure patients will remain who have not succeeded in incorporating the therapist within their own psyche, and who do continue to need to have the therapist, or some substitute for him, as an actual person in the external world to whom they feel that they can have recourse when this is really needed. 'Chronic' patients of this kind are at least as common in ordinary medical practice. My way of dealing with such patients has been to see them at ever-increasing intervals; once every three, or even every six, months. This has been a sheet anchor which has enabled a few such patients to manage their lives without recourse to other supportive agencies. Their knowledge that I am still available has meant that they have not had to make use of my availability; and the fact that they have been able to see me occasionally has reassured them of my continuing existence and interest.

Some patients, usually those of obsessional personality, tend to persist with therapy indefinitely because they feel that there is still more fascinating exploration to be undertaken, and that, 'had we but world enough and time', additional enthralling revelations and profounder insights would be obtained. Patients can become 'stuck' in psychotherapy in the same way, as Jung observed, that they become 'stuck' in neurosis. It is possible to make the therapeutic situation a substitute for life; and it is not only patients who fall into this trap. There are therapists also who have virtually no life outside their hours of practice.

As I have already stated, the results of psychotherapy are very difficult to assess, partly because of the change in emphasis from treating symptoms to understanding persons as a whole, and partly because changes in attitude are intrinsically difficult to measure. In the early fifties, Hans Eysenck began his on-slaught upon psychoanalysis and derivative forms of psychotherapy by suggesting that there was no hard evidence that such forms of treatment had any value. In subsequent years, he sharpened his attack by quoting statistics which pur-ported to show that, in neurosis, spontaneous remission within a period of about two years was as frequent, or rather more frequent, than recovery following psychotherapy. In subse-quent years, considerable doubt was thrown upon Eysenck's handling and interpretation of the figures available to him[15]; and the latest available evidence shows quite clearly that he was wrong. If a person is suffering from a neurosis, he is more likely to recover if he seeks professional help from a psychotherapist than if he merely waits for his troubles to pass. Moreover, as techniques of assessment are refined, psychotherapy is found to be more effective rather than less. Thus, in a later edition of a well-known book, the authors are able to write; 'In contrast to the chapter on this topic in the previous edition of the *Hand-book*, wherein it was concluded that psychotherapy had an average effect that was modestly positive, recent outcome data look more favorable. A growing number of controlled outcome studies are analysing a wide variety of therapies. These findings generally yield clearly positive results when compared with no treatment, wait-list, and placebo or pseudotherapies . . . Our review of the empirical assessment of a broad range of verbal psychotherapies leads us to conclude that these methods are worthwhile when practised by wise and stable therapists.'[16] Another well-known book of similar status goes further. 'In the opinion of the majority of practitioners, of patients who have received treatment, and of unprejudiced observers, psycho-therapy, properly instituted, is the most effective measure available to us today for the treatment of emotional problems and for the liberation of potential adaptive and creative resources in the individual.'[17]

I think it likely that, as we become more skilled in our selection of patients for psychotherapy, and as other methods of treatment are developed for those who are not judged suitable, our results will improve still further. Psychotherapy has suf-fered both from the over-enthusiasm of some practitioners, and also from the fact that so little could be done for many classes of psychiatric patient that psychotherapy was sometimes embarked upon as a last resort. This still happens today. Although those who are beginning the practice of psychotherapy do not usually have much say in the selection of patients who are referred to them, they should beware of those consultants who unload their difficult patients upon them without attempting to judge their suitability. Very often, the fact that this is taking place will be revealed by the bulkiness of the casenotes, which indicates that every other method of treatment has probably been tried. Consultants who behave like this are usually those who have little experience of psychotherapy themselves, and no belief in its efficacy.

In an early paper, Freud attempted, tentatively, to indicate the conditions under which psychoanalysis was indicated or contra-indicated. He begins by writing: 'One should look beyond the patient's illness and form an estimate of his whole personality; those patients who do not possess a reasonable degree of education and a fairly reliable character should be refused. It must not be forgotten that there are healthy people as well as unhealthy ones who are good for nothing in life, and that there is a temptation to ascribe to their illness everything that incapacitates them, if they show any sign of neurosis. . . .' He goes on to reject as unsuitable patients who have been pressed into seeking help by relatives; a problem I touched on in Chapter 3. He also makes the point that when the patient is suffering from dangerous symptoms like severe anorexia, psychoanalysis is inappropriate. 'To be quite safe', Freud alleges, 'one should limit one's choice of patients to those who possess a normal mental condition, since in the psychoanalytic method this is used as a foothold from which to obtain control of the morbid manifestations. Psychoses, states of confusion and deeply-rooted (I might say toxic) depression are therefore not suitable for psychoanalysis; at least not for the method as it has been practised up to the present. I do not regard it as by any means impossible that by suitable changes in the method we may succeed in overcoming this contra-indication – and so be able to initiate a psychotherapy of the psychoses.' In this early paper Freud also rejects patients of fifty and over; but in this he has been shown to be too gloomy, since many older people respond quite satisfactorily to psychotherapy.[18]

If Freud's original indications had been observed, there would be less argument than there has been about the efficacy of analytic forms of psychotherapy; but enthusiasts have attempted to treat all manner of unsuitable persons, including psychotics, of whom very few are suitable, and psychopaths and criminals, who seldom respond to any type of psychotherapy. Even sexual perverts, who are often referred to psychotherapists, may not always be suitable for this variety of treatment. Fairbairn, in an interesting and neglected paper on 'The Treatment and Rehabilitation of Sexual Offenders'[19] deplores what he calls 'a widespread movement among psychiatrists towards the point of view that perverse sexual tendencies are 'symptoms' in the same sense as those which characterise the psychoneuroses. He recalls Freud's remark that neurosis is the negative of perversion, and also his statement that psychoneurotic symptoms are essentially defensive in character. Fairbairn goes on to state that 'when perverse sexual tendencies are present in a psychoneurotic, these are subject to drastic measures of control at the hands of a powerful part of the personality'. Fairbairn makes it clear that he does not consider that individual psychotherapy is the most suitable treatment for those who, like sexual offenders, fail to exercise control over their impulses. What such people need, in Fairbairn's view, is rehabilitation rather than treatment; and by this he means an integration into society of such a kind that they accept society's standards of behaviour, and therefore no longer 'act out' their impulses. I think Fairbairn would have welcomed a behavioural approach to the problems posed by sexual offenders.[19]

Psychotherapists seem to me to be best at treating the inhibited, the frightened, the shy, the self-distrustful, the fragmented, the over-dependent, and the over-controlled. They are far less successful with those who lack control over their impulses, and who 'act out' their emotional conflicts. Patients who show disturbances like over- or under-eating; who drink too much, or who smoke compulsively; who steal, who drive dangerously, or who commit sexual offences or other criminal acts, are poor bets for individual psychotherapy. For some, behaviour therapy offers a better chance of bringing abnormal behaviour under control. For others, there is no substitute for a long process of socialisation within a closed community. We do a disservice to psychotherapy if we pretend that it is applicable to a wider range of disorders than those in which we know it to be effective. For these, in my opinion, it is unsurpassed and irreplaceable.

References

1. Breuer, Josef and Freud, Sigmund (1893) *Studies on Hysteria*. Standard Edition Collected Works, Vol. 2, p. 6. London: Hogarth Press (1955).
2. Freud, Sigmund (1895) *Obsessions and Phobias*. Standard Edition Collected Works, Vol. 3, p. 77. London: Hogarth Press (1962).
3. Freud, Sigmund (1933) *New Introductory Lectures on Psycho-Analysis*. Standard Edition Collected Works, Vol. 22, p. 156. London: Hogarth Press (1964).
4. Rycroft, Charles (1962) Beyond the Reality Principle. *Int. J. Psycho-Anal.*, 43.
5. Freud, Sigmund (1940) *An Outline of Psycho-Analysis*. Standard Edition Collected Works, Vol. 23, p. 184. London: Hogarth Press (1964).
6. Fenichel, Otto (1945) *The Psychoanalytic Theory of Neurosis*, p. 19. New York: W. W. Norton.
7. Jung, C. G. (1931) 'The Aims of Psychotherapy' in *The Practice of Psychotherapy*, Collected Works, Vol. 16, pp. 41, 42, 47. London: Routledge and Kegan Paul (1954).
8. Rogers, Carl (1967) *On becoming a Person*, pp. 171–2. London: Constable.
9. Szasz, Thomas (1965) *The Ethics of Psychoanalysis*, pp. viii–ix. New York: Basic Books.
10. Rogers, Carl (1967) *On becoming a Person*, p. 175. London: Constable.
11. Rogers, Carl (1967) *On becoming a Person*, p. 167. London: Constable.
12. Fairbairn, W. R. D. (1958) 'On the Nature and Aims of Psychoanalytical Treatment.' *Int. J. Psycho-Anal.*, **39,** part 5.

13.   Reich, Annie (1950) *Int. J. Psycho-Anal.*, **31**: 78–80, 179–205. Quoted in Wolberg, Lewis R. (1977) *The Technique of Psychotherapy*, Part Two, Third Edition. New York: Grune and Stratton.

14.   Frank, Jerome (1969) *Persuasion and Healing*, Chapter 11. New York: Schocken Books.

15.   Brown, Roger and Herrnstein, Richard J. (1975) *Psychology*, pp. 596–7. London: Methuen.

16.   Garfield, Sol L. and Bergin, Allen E. (1978) *Handbook of Psychotherapy and Behavior Change*, pp. 179–80. New York: John Wiley.

17.   Wolberg, Lewis R. (1977) *The Technique of Psychotherapy*, Part One. p. 67, New York: Grune and Stratton.

18.   Freud, Sigmund (1904) *On Psychotherapy* Standard Edition, Collected Works, Vol. 7, pp. 263–4. London: Hogarth Press (1953).

19.   Fairbairn, W. Ronald D. (1946) 'The Treatment and Rehabilitation of Sexual Offenders' in *Psychoanalytic Studies of the Personality*. London: Tavistock (1952).

14

The Personality of the Psychotherapist

Since individual psychotherapy depends upon an interaction between two personalities, it follows that we ought to make some attempt to understand the personality of the psychotherapist. In this chapter, I want to consider what kind of person is attracted toward the practice of psychotherapy and why. I shall also have something to say about the effects of practising psychotherapy upon the therapist. Are those who are attracted toward the profession the best kind of people to become psychotherapists? And are there some who should be discouraged or prevented from pursuing this branch of psychiatry?

In my submission, the traits of personality which attract people toward becoming psychotherapists are deep-rooted, just as are those which determine other choices of occupation demanding special qualities. It is unlikely that peculiarities of personality are important factors determining whether a man becomes a shop assistant, a farm labourer, or a milk-roundsman. But whether or not a man becomes an artist, a scientist, a philosopher or a priest is determined less by accident than by his possessing a particular combination of gifts and temperamental traits. I believe the same to be true of the psychotherapist. Moreover, some of the personality characteristics required by psychotherapists are double-edged. The traits that go to make a good therapist may be disadvantageous in other spheres. Habitual attitudes which are appropriate in the consulting-room may not be so elsewhere. Every type of temperament which is at all strongly defined is bound to have both advantages and disadvantages and that which distinguishes many psychotherapists is no exception.

The man in the street generally regards psychotherapy as an eccentric occupation. Most people have a rather limited capacity for sympathy with the troubles of others, and find it inconceivable that anyone, all day and every day, should choose to listen to stories of distress. Some imagine that, were they in the shoes of the psychotherapist, they would become intensely impatient; others that they would succumb to despair. In their eyes, the psychotherapist is regarded either as mentally ill himself, or else as a kind of secular saint who is able to rise above ordinary human limitations. Neither view is true. Although some psychotherapists are eccentric, others are not notably so, and none, in my experience, is a saint. Are psychotherapists particularly neurotic? Most will admit that their interest in the subject took origin from their own emotional problems; but this is too banal and general a statement to be illuminating. There can be few intelligent adolescents who have not read something about psychology in the hope of understanding themselves better, and the fact that psychotherapists have often done the same does not tell us much about them. I once had a conversation with the director of a monastery. 'Everyone who comes to us', he said, 'does so for the wrong reasons.' The same is generally true of people who become psychotherapists. It is sometimes possible to persuade people to become psychotherapists who have not chosen the profession for their own personal reasons; but, for the most part, we have to put up with what we can get; namely, ourselves. However, it is not simply because they want to understand themselves better that people take up psychotherapy professionally. It is because certain features of their personalities make the practice of psychotherapy rewarding. I shall first try to depict what seem to me to be some of the personality traits displayed by those who seem to be successful psychotherapists, and then consider what may be the psychopathology of such traits; their possible origin, their advantages and disadvantages.

It is obvious that psychotherapists must be 'interested in people'; that is, in the world of the personal rather than the impersonal. In my experience, most psychotherapists, whether medically qualified or not, are not primarily scientists. There is a considerable body of work which points to the fact that people who are attracted toward the exact sciences and those who are drawn toward the arts and humanities differ in temperament, and that this difference manifests itself early in life. From Liam Hudson's research, it appears that potential scientists tend to show little capacity for introspection, or for emotional response to others. They make a sharp distinction between their private lives and their professional activities, and are usually rather conventional in social behaviour. Those who are attracted by the arts, in contrast, show a greater capacity for introspection; react more emotionally toward others; make little separation between their work and their private lives; and take longer than scientists to settle down and achieve stability in life. Liam Hudson notes that popular imagination associates ideas of pleasure with artists, ideas of value with scientists. 'Artist, poet and novelist are all seen in my studies as warm and exciting, but as of little worth. Mathematicians, physicists, and engineers are all seen as extremely valuable, but also as dull and cold.'[1] There is reason to think that those who become scientists are temperamentally governed by the notion of self-control, whilst those who turn toward the arts are more influenced by the idea of self-expression.

Another way of putting this is to say that scientists are equipped with a better mechanism of repression by which they tend to exclude the emotional and the irrational from their experience; and that this partly determines their choice of an occupation which requires the greatest possible objectivity and elimination of the personal. I think it is clear that the good psychotherapist is likely to fall on the arts side of the line, and that this is appropriate. Research into the personalities of therapists has suggested that 'Therapists effective with neurotics like literature and art.'[2] As we have seen, results in psychotherapy are difficult to quantify; but temperamental characteristics also partly account for the lack of interest in quantification shown by psychotherapists; a trait which has brought them into disrepute with experimental psychologists. Although psychotherapists must be capable of a certain degree of detachment and objectivity, they, like those who choose the arts and humanities, must seek to experience and include the emotional and irrational. Openness toward one's own emotions and openness toward the emotions of others go hand-in-hand; and so the psychotherapist is attracted toward work in which the expression of emotion is not forbidden, but actually encouraged; and in which he has the opportunity of reaching a better understanding of his own emotions as well as those of his patients.

I wrote in Chapter 13 that when psychotherapy becomes concerned with understanding persons rather than with abolishing symptoms, it cannot be a scientific enterprise. Psychotherapists who guiltily feel that they are not as 'scientific' as their medical colleagues in other specialities can comfort themselves with the reflection that, if they were so, they would not be any good at their job. Carl Rogers wrote in one of his books: 'There are also many whose concept of the individual is that of an object to be dissected, diagnosed, manipulated. Such professional workers may find it very difficult to learn or to practise a client-centred form of psychotherapy.'[3]

The radical behaviourists, of whom B. F. Skinner is the most famous example, take precisely this attitude to human beings; and, although their way of thinking is no longer seriously entertained by academic psychologists, their claim that behaviourism is the only truly scientific way of understanding human beings has left its mark. Skinner, it will be recalled, has a notion of Utopia in which the environment is so controlled that appropriate 'contingencies of reinforcement' will automatically produce socially desirable behaviour and general happiness. Skinner writes: 'What is being abolished is autonomous man – the inner man . . . the man defended by the literatures of freedom and dignity. His abolition has long been overdue . . . A scientific analysis of behaviour dispossesses autonomous man and turns the control he has been said to exert over to the environment . . . What is needed is more control, not less . . . The problem is to design a world which will be liked not by people as they now are but by those who live in it . . . It is science or nothing . . .'.[4]

But the attitude which treats human beings as objects which can be scientifically manipulated and controlled in the same way in which inanimate objects can be manipulated and controlled, robs the human being of autonomy, is impossible to sustain in social life, and actually deprives the observer of an important source of understanding of his fellow-men. Although those who have been trained in the tradition of the exact sciences would like to see the difference abolished, there really is a sense in which understanding another person is different from understanding a disease, an animal, or a tree. Isaiah Berlin makes the point with his customary clarity in his book, *Vico and Herder*.

'Understanding other men's motives or acts, however imperfect or corrigible, is a state of mind or activity in principle different from learning about, or knowledge of, the external world.

'Just as we can say with assurance that we ourselves are not only bodies in space, acted upon by measurable natural forces, but that we think, choose, follow rules, make decisions, in other words, possess an inner life of which we are aware and which we can describe, so we take for granted — and, if questioned, say that we are certain — that others possess a similar inner life, without which the notion of communication, or language, or of human society, as opposed to an aggregate of human bodies, becomes unintelligible.'[5]

Understanding other human beings, therefore, requires that the observer does not simply note their behaviour as if they were machines or totally different from himself, but demands that he make use of his own understanding of himself, his own feelings, thoughts, intentions, and motives in order to understand others.

This kind of understanding, as Isaiah Berlin implies, is a refinement and deepening of the kind of understanding which we employ every day in our social lives, and without which social life would be impossible. To adopt an impersonal, scientific attitude to human beings tells us only about their behaviour; it is to treat them as not possessing an inner life, more particularly, as not possessing will or intention. D. C. Dennett, in his essay on *Mechanism and Responsibility*, refers to 'intentional explanations' which 'cite thoughts, desires, beliefs, intentions, rather than chemical reactions, explosions, electric impulses, in explaining the occurrences of human motions'.[6] The impersonal, scientific stance (referred to by Dennett as 'mechanistic') can only inform us about another person's behaviour; and although, by adopting this attitude, we may be able to discern *causes* for this behaviour, our explanation cannot be in terms of intention, nor can we determine what this behaviour *means* to the individual concerned.

In our ordinary day-to-day encounters with individuals, we are bound to adopt the intentional stance. I cannot but assume that I myself have feelings, desires, thoughts, beliefs, and intentions, and, in the ordinary way, inevitably assume that others are similarly constituted. In *Fights, Games and Debates*, Anatol Rapoport[7] points out that when we are playing a game, we are bound to make what he calls 'the assumption of similarity' about our opponent; that is, that he intends to win if he can, and that, in trying to do so, he will be influenced by the same sort of considerations, and have in mind the same kinds of strategy as we do ourselves. If we could not make the assumption of similarity, games would be impossible, and so, in fact, would social life.

The skills which the psychotherapist must develop, therefore, depend upon reciprocal understanding. The more he learns about himself, the more will he be able to understand his patients. The more he learns about his patients, the more will he be able to understand himself.

Good psychotherapists must not only be interested in people, but also possess the capacity for empathy with a wide range of different types of personality. We all have our limitations; and no-one can empathise with every kind of person. But psychotherapists must have an interest in people who, at first sight, may not resemble themselves or share their interests. I think this capacity is also connected with a relative absence of repression. For it is when one can recognise that embryonic features of the same emotional problems with which the patient is struggling are present in oneself that one can begin to empathise with what the patient is feeling; and this capacity, I believe, argues that one has not, too early in life, excluded from consciousness, and from what one conceives to be one's own character, possibilities that one might have developed entirely differently. This includes, for example, the possibility that one might have become an exact scientist, with the capacity for repression which that implies. Perhaps one can fully understand only those aspects of personality in others of which one can find traces in oneself. The fact that psychotherapy demands a kind of flexibility toward oneself as well as toward the patient has its disadvantages, as I shall later discuss.

Openness toward emotion should imply that psychotherapists display an unusual tolerance of emotional expression in others. If someone starts to shed tears, many people become embarrassed, angry, or feel at a loss and run away from the situation. Psychotherapists, on the other hand, need to be able to facilitate the expression of distress on the part of the patient without themselves becoming so distressed that they want to escape. It is important that patients be allowed to weep without the therapist immediately trying to stop them. A good deal of conventional comforting is as much aimed at relieving the distress of the comforter as that of the sufferer. Therapists must also be capable of facilitating the expression of anger, even when it may be directed toward themselves; another feature of psychotherapy which the layman finds hard to understand. A tolerant awareness of one's own angry potential is essential if this is to be accomplished.

Although the psychotherapist needs to be aware of his own feelings if he is to understand those of the patient, he must not use the psychotherapeutic session as a forum for displaying them. In Chapter 7 I indicated why it was inadvisable for the therapist to talk intimately to the patient about himself. This is not to say that the therapist should try to be detached or cold. Psychotherapists need to be affected by their patients' emotions if they are to understand them; and the fact that they do understand will manifest itself in their manner and tone of voice, without their competing with the patient in emotional display. This requires considerable control and self-abnegation on the part of the therapist. It is easy for intellectual, remote persons to tolerate the emotions of others; they do so by detachment and avoidance. It is easy for warm, sympathetic human beings to enter into another's distress; to proffer tea, sympathy, or love, and to share with the other person their own, not dissimilar experience. The therapist's task is more difficult. He has to be affected without acting upon his own feelings: to feel, but to use his own feelings in the service of the patient, as a guide to understanding, not as a way of demonstrating how kind, how loving, how sympathetic he himself is. Only thus will he be able to help the patient better to understand and to master his own emotional problems.

The capacity for self-abnegation, for not using such situations for personal ends is essential and, I think, unusual. It is, I believe, more often found in women than in men. In the U.S.A. Margaret Rioch, a clinical psychologist, instituted a programme of training for married women whose children were about to leave home and who were looking for a new occupation, but who had not considered practising psychotherapy as a possibility. This programme has been successful; and opens the way to recruiting a new kind of therapist; one who has not been driven to seek training in psychotherapy on account of her own need for help.[8]

It is certainly one of the more peculiar features of the practice of psychotherapy that the therapist spends the bulk of his professional life in situations in which his own self-expression is forbidden, or at least severely restricted. If one compares the life of a psychotherapist with that of a politician, a journalist, a teacher, or a barrister, this restriction is evident. It is less manifest in comparison with the lives of medical practitioners or solicitors, who ought also to be governed more by their clients' needs than by any desire to express themselves directly; but it is still more restricted than those. Much more than any other professional, the psychotherapist, whilst on the job, needs to be less than normally self-assertive; if not an enigma, at least not a completely known quantity. His own personality is never fully expressed, but always orientated toward the needs of the other.

Closely related with the capacity for self-abnegation is another important trait. This may be described as a reluctance on the part of the therapist to take over, to give orders, or to seek immediate practical solutions to problems. There is some evidence from research to support this opinion. 'Neurotics are not well served by therapists who like to solve problems', alleges James K. Dent,[9] from whose work I have already quoted. Parker found that 'therapists who tended to dominate their clients and to respond to them in a directive manner were less successful than those who did not in bringing about client statements indicative of understanding and insight'.[10]

It is difficult for people who are natural leaders, who enjoy telling others what to do, to become good psychotherapists. The opposite is also true. In *The Psychology of Human Communication*, John Parry writes: 'It has been said of two British Prime Ministers that one possessed no antennae, while the other possessed nothing else. If by antennae we understand alertness to nuance and undertone, it is easy to see how either tendency can lead to failure in business and government. The man who is all perception is likely to reflect the prevailing mood without adding direction of his own; the leader deaf to the moods and feelings of others may produce clear-cut plans but will be unable to gauge their acceptability.'[11] Either tendency can lead to failure in psychotherapy in that the therapist with antennae can so identify himself with the patient's experience that he, like the patient, is unable critically to distance himself from that experience: but this is less common than the failure which arises from the therapist's lack of perception.

Before the days of Freud, psychotherapists were often authoritarian and didactic; more like ordinary doctors. Freud himself began by treating neurotics with hypnosis; a treatment which, originally, depended upon the prestige and authority of the therapist in conjunction with the passivity and acquiescence of the patient. Freud did not finally abandon hypnosis until 1896; but, during the years from 1892 onwards, he was gradually modifying his technique.

He gave up using symptoms as starting-points in sessions, and ceased persuading or urging patients to recall apparently forgotten memories. Instead, he substituted the technique of free association; and I think it is arguable that this handing over the lead to the patient with a consequent alteration in the role of the doctor is the greatest of Freud's discoveries.

The training of psychotherapists ought to reinforce their disinclination to be authoritarian, in that their task is usually presented as one of helping the patient to help himself rather than telling him what to do, or proffering direct assistance. To be able habitually to behave in this way with patients argues a degree of passivity on the part of the therapist, which may be why one seldom finds psychotherapists as heads of departments. Their lack of overt aggression may, of course, mask considerable aggressiveness within; but its absence as an easily accessible ego-function is noticeable in people drawn to psychotherapy as a profession, who prefer to exercise power in ways which do not require quick decision, giving orders, or any other form of acting directly or assertively upon the world and the persons round them.

It is now well established that psychotherapists need to be capable of genuine concern and warmth toward their patients. Research, quite apart from common sense, has shown that warm acceptance facilitates personality change, just as criticism tends to arouse hostility, and therefore makes change more difficult. Psychotherapists must, of course, say critical things from time to time; but, if the patient feels that the therapist is unequivocally on his side, it is astonishing how well he will be able to accept a critical assessment of his attitudes and relationships. My phrase 'unequivocally on his side' may be taken as equivalent to Rogers' 'unconditional positive regard'; perhaps the most powerful of all therapeutic factors in psychotherapy. Psychotherapists should be especially able to extend positive regard toward those whom the world has rejected. Successful therapists, I think, generally possess an especial capacity for identifying with the insulted and injured. This capacity is seldom possessed by the general run of mankind, who, even if not contemptuous of, or impatient with, those who feel neurotically ill-at-ease in the world, do not find it easy to display especial compassion toward them.

Psychotherapists often have some personal knowledge of what it is like to feel insulted and injured, a kind of knowledge which they might rather be without, but which actually extends the range of their compassion. Freud himself experienced ridicule and hostility during the earlier part of his life, and, in old age, had to flee Vienna in order to escape from Nazi persecution. Many of his followers also became refugees. The experience of being rejected by one's fellows, whether for reasons of race, or because of personal difficulties in making peer relationships in childhood may leave the individual with a curious mixture of hostility and suspicion directed toward ordinary people combined with an especial compassion with those whom he feels have been rejected like himself. It is a mixture which I think I have often detected in the personalities of psychotherapists.

Ideally, psychotherapists should be, and often are, persons of wide sympathies who are open both to their own emotions and to those of others: able to identify with a wide range of people; tolerant of the expression of both grief and rage; warm and sympathetic without being sentimental; predominantly non-assertive, but capable of quietly maintaining their own position: able to put themselves at the patient's service, and to accept that their reward for doing so may be both long-delayed and indirect. This picture may sound too good to be true; but if we study the psychopathology which I believe to be associated with it, it will no longer appear so.

A psychoanalyst who has had as patients or trainees rather a large number of psychotherapists once remarked to me that he had found a good many of them to have had depressed mothers. I have no statistics which would prove or disprove this statement, but if it were true, it would not surprise me. Sensitivity toward the feelings of others is an essential part of the psychotherapist's equipment; and such sensitivity can, I believe, generally be traced to the circumstances of the therapist's childhood. Why should it be necessary for a child to develop a particularly sensitive awareness of what others are feeling? Often, I think, because such sensitivity springs from an anxiety not to upset or anger or distress one or both parents. Suppose, for example, that a child has a particularly irritable, difficult father. He will surely learn to watch out for danger signals; to be more than usually alert to what might upset his father; to study the father's wishes, and comply with them, in order to avoid arousing wrath.

Or suppose that the child's mother is ailing or low-spirited. He will have to learn not to make demands upon his mother, and will also become sensitive to what factors seem to make her tired or ill or depressed. This anxious awareness of what may upset parents may inhibit natural, spontaneous behaviour, and sometimes has the result of making the child feel that his demands are selfish, illegitimate, or even potentially harmful. Instead of a freely expressed demand which a parent might as freely either meet or refuse, such a child may come to feel that his own need for love is likely to be destructive. Moreover, if he comes to feel that his own needs and demands are bad, he will be left with an anxiety as to whether he is likeable or lovable, and an especial need to prove that he is so. This will reinforce his tendency to be over-anxious to please, or even ingratiating. No-one likes to be labelled ingratiating; but anxiety to please and sensitivity to what may be upsetting to others are useful traits which help the psychotherapist to make an initial contact with patients who begin by being hostile or suspicious.

If we follow the consequences of this presumed psychopathology a little further, we shall see that it links in with other features of the psychotherapist's personality. For, if a child's behaviour is governed by anxiety over the effects which his demands may have upon his parents, he is, it is clear, relegating himself to second place. He is giving precedence to his parents' needs. A child of this kind might, therefore, grow up to be an adult who is not only sensitively orientated towards what others are feeling, but who also has a tendency toward self-abnegation and putting others first.

This attitude also has the effect of encouraging repression of the child's aggressive feelings; since self-assertion is forbidden, and self-assertion cannot be separated from aggression. I do not think that anyone can be primarily orientated toward the feelings of others without repressing considerable aggression. Psychotherapists, therefore, are not so 'nice' as they sometimes appear; a trait which did not escape the notice of Freud, who thought that therapeutic enthusiasm was a defence against sadism. During their training, I believe that many of those in the 'helping' professions have, reluctantly, to face and accept an aggressive aspect of their personalities which they might not have realised existed. If they succeed in doing so, it will be easier for them to tolerate any aggression which patients may display toward them, and easier for them to assert their own opinions and needs in social life, where this is appropriate.

Lack of self-assertion seems to go hand-in-hand with some uncertainty about identity. There is a tendency for psychotherapists to be all things to all men, and hence to lack firmness, consistency, and definiteness of personality; qualities which we usually associate with those we admire. If a therapist is constantly orientated toward understanding others rather than toward expressing his own views, those views may never be explicitly or firmly formulated. It is desirable that therapists should be as free as possible of prejudice, although this is an ideal impossible of attainment. But lack of prejudice may also reflect a lack of genuine conviction, of any formed, positive attitude toward the world.

However, there is one sphere in which a somewhat fluid sense of identity is a positive advantage. It is desirable that psychotherapists should not identify themselves too closely with the sexual stereotypes operating in whatever society they live in. They must be capable of receiving both the masculine and the feminine projections of their patients; to be both 'mother' and 'father'. If the therapist is too markedly feminine, or too obviously masculine, it is more difficult for the patient to project both kinds of image. Projections need hooks to which to attach themselves. It is also valuable for the therapist to be able to identify with either sex; to imagine what it would be like to be the opposite sex. This implies being aware of one's own contrasexual traits. It is interesting that, in studies of creative men, psychologists have consistently reported high scores on tests measuring femininity. The greatest novelists, of whom Tolstoy is the supreme example, can identify with, and depict, the opposite sex with entire conviction. It is interesting that Tolstoy, who found difficulty in controlling his very powerful sexual drive, never achieved a consistent, firm identity. All his life, he alternated between sensuality and asceticism, arrogance and humility, idealism and cynicism. His lack of consistency may have contributed to his achievement as a novelist, but made him extremely difficult to live with. The same may be true of some psychotherapists.

Persons who are attracted to the practice of psychotherapy often seem to relate to others by identification with the other rather than by mutual self-affirmation on equal terms. Whilst a large measure of identification with the patient may be necessary within the therapeutic setting, it is undesirable in relationships with friends, although an easy way of being initially accepted by them. It is tempting, but wrong, for the psychotherapist to take into social life a way of relating to people which is more appropriate to the consulting room. Most people are only too willing to talk at length about themselves, and, since therapists are, or ought to be, experts at 'drawing people out', some of their social encounters may consist of a monologue on the part of the person with whom they are talking, with the therapist making no more contribution than he would when a patient was freely associating. Although such a conversation may leave the other participant with a conviction that he has been talking to someone particularly 'nice', he may, on reflection, recall that the therapist has not said anything about himself, and that he therefore had had no real opportunity of judging whether he was nice or not. There are a number of ruthlessly narcissistic people for whom the monologue is a substitute for conversation; but most of those who are less self-absorbed do regard social encounters as an opportunity for interchange on more or less equal terms. After being trapped into a monologue, such a person may rightly conclude that the therapist's apparent modesty was actually a devious way of putting himself in the superior position, reminiscent of those catalogued by the late Stephen Potter.

The fact that people who are attracted to the practice of psychotherapy tend to relate to others by identification rather than by mutual self-affirmation on equal terms has the consequence that the desire for power which they share with others is somewhat muted, and may not be obvious either to their patients or to themselves. Although psychotherapists put their personalities and skills at the service of their patients, they are, in reality, in an exceptionally powerful position. First, they are in a position where they may either graciously condescend to 'take on' the patient, or else refuse to do so. Since psychotherapists have been in short supply in this country, psychotherapy has been a seller's market for many years; and some analysts, although charging very high fees, have not scrupled to make the patient feel that he is fortunate in being allowed to recline on their particular couch. Since one of the objects of psychotherapy is to help those who are immature and uncertain of themselves attain a conviction of their own equality with other men, such an attitude on the part of the therapist is not conducive to the patient's recovery. It is also gratifying, though often worrying, to have patients who are very dependent upon one, a fact to which I drew attention in Chapter 7; and some therapists who are particularly unaware of their own desire for power may, unconsciously in most cases, but not in all, encourage dependency by failing to make manifest the patient's dependency or encourage him to overcome it. This is obviously more likely to happen in private practice, especially if the patient is well-off and settles his accounts promptly. Psychotherapists may not exercise power in an obvious, direct fashion; but they are *eminences grises* who have more power than some of them realise; and the temptation to abuse this power is something of which psychotherapists should constantly remind themselves. What I have just written applies to all those in the 'helping' professions to a lesser extent.

I wrote above that psychotherapists have been, and still are, in short supply. This obviously raises the question of whether some of those who take up this profession do so because they realise this, whilst fearing that they might fail at anything more competitive. There may be a few instances of such hard-headed calculation, but I think such people are uncommon. As I hope I have indicated, the personality traits which draw people toward psychotherapy originate in childhood, before considerations of how to make a living are as important as they become in later life.

Sensitivity toward the feelings of others combined with the repression of self-assertive tendencies may not, in childhood, be a mixture of traits conducive to ease in mixing with peers. Children of both sexes need to be sufficiently overtly 'aggressive' to stand up for themselves. I have the impression that a number of those who become psychotherapists do so not only because sensitivity and an absence of self-assertion are traits which are useful in practice, but because their early difficulties in mixing have led them to choose a structured situation in which conventions and rules govern the interchange and in which intimacy is of necessity one-sided. Provided that the therapist is aware of how his own psychopathology has contributed to his choice of profession, he can make use of it in the constructive way which, I wrote in Chapter 13, was what we should help our patients to achieve. Indeed, without some of the traits I have outlined, the potential therapist would neither be attracted toward the profession, nor be any good at it once he had adopted it.

However, there are two types of person who sometimes become psychotherapists who do so for reasons even more 'wrong' than the ones I have outlined. In his book *Anxiety and Neurosis*, Charles Rycroft writes: 'Obsessional characters are often attracted to psychology, since it seems to hold out the possibility of knowing about and therefore being able to control precisely those aspects of themselves and others which are most elusive and unpredictable. They find psychological theories which ignore intuition, which rely on statistical analyses, and which include the idea or ideal of 'normality' particularly fascinating, since they encourage the notion that emotions can be mastered intellectually and that there is a known and desirable pattern of behaviour to which one can adjust oneself — thereby enabling them to feel that it is always possible to tread on safe and familiar territory.

'They are also attracted by philosophical systems since they create the illusion that it might be possible to discover a key to the universe which would enable one to understand everything in general and thus become immune to anxiety-provoking encounters with unknown particulars.'[12]

Although the first part of Rycroft's statement may more usually be applied to those who are attracted by experimental psychology, a group of people who, in this country, generally repudiate psychotherapists and all their works, there are a few psychotherapists who, unfortunately, do correspond to this description. They include some who appear to have no antennae, no trace whatever of any understanding either of themselves or of others, and who are drawn to psychotherapy because they believe, quite wrongly, that its practice will dispel the mists of their unperceptiveness.

The latter part of Rycroft's statement, that concerned with philosophical systems, more fittingly applies to those analysts who elevate their particular 'school' into a dogmatic faith; and who believe that only they, and a few other chosen spirits, preferably analysed by themselves, have any deep understanding of human nature. Such are the analysts who believe in some mythical ideal of being 'completely analysed', and who denigrate those who do not subscribe to their beliefs as being insufficiently trained (they mean 'converted'); who create splinter groups within analytic institutions, and who entirely fail to recognise that, in a relatively new discipline to which many and various types of mind may each have something to contribute, dogmatism is both out of place and a sign of their own insecurity. Analysts of this kind have not, in Kleinian terminology, advanced beyond the paranoid-schizoid position to acquire the capacity for being depressed. For is not a characteristic of the paranoid personality to *know* that he is right and that others are wrong, whilst the person who has reached the depressive position is more easily able to doubt whether he himself or anyone else has the only key to understanding human beings? Inexperienced psychotherapists tend to be over-awed by those with strong convictions. I would recommend that they read *The Pursuit of the Millennium* by Norman Cohn,[13] which is a learned exposé of the paranoid nature of sectarian movements. These invariably display three features: a leader who is sure that he is right and who makes promises of future bliss: an enemy, be it the Establishment, Anti-Christ, or anyone else who does not subscribe to the doctrine being promulgated; and a group of followers who for reasons connected either with external circumstances or with their own psychology, are sufficiently at a disadvantage or insecure enough to need to become attached to such a leader.

I have outlined some of the psychological characteristics which distinguish at least a number of those who are attracted toward the practice of psychotherapy. This outline is partly based on introspection, and partly on knowledge of other psychotherapists, either as patients or colleagues. I hope that what I have written goes some way to answering the naive question of whether psychotherapists are as neurotic, or even need to be as neurotic, as those whom they purport to treat. I believe that neurosis is more a matter of being overwhelmed by, or at the mercy of, one's psychopathology than of possessing any particular pattern of psychopathology. I think it is clear that those who are going through some crisis, or who are partially overwhelmed by their personal problems, are not likely to be able to give the kind of attention to the problems of others which is required of the psychotherapist. On the other hand, those who think that they have no personal problems at all are still more unsuitable. Mental health is not to be defined as absence of problems. The only persons who have no problems are those that are dead, or else so rigid and so unaware of themselves that they have ceased to develop. I suggested earlier that psychotherapists are more like artists than scientists. One characteristic of creative people who work in the arts is that they continue to change and develop, and are constantly tackling new problems. Those that do not cease to produce anything of interest. Directly one attains a rigid point of view, an absolute certainty in life, in which one has the illusion of being free of problems, one loses the capacity for personal growth, and also the capacity to identify with others and understand their problems. Since we all tend toward increasing rigidity as we grow older, it is arguable that psychotherapy is better practised by the young; and it is true that both Freud and Jung, as they became elderly, tended to lose interest in therapy, and to show more interest in problems of theory. However, we may take courage from the example shown by some of the great creators, who continued to change and develop into extreme old age. Verdi, for example, wrote *Falstaff* when he was eighty; an opera which, in many respects, is a new departure. Michelangelo, who was almost eighty-nine when he died, was working on the Rondanini Pietà six days before his death; and this, too, is a new departure, a paring down to essentials. These great men had problems; problems of integration, of striving after a yet more perfect manner of expression; problems which were not just matters of technique, but closely bound up with the fact that they themselves were developing and changing, right up to their deaths. They did not know all the answers; they never arrived, but always continued to travel hopefully. This, I think, should be the attitude which the psychotherapist should have, both to his own problems and to those of others.

I am often asked by pupils whether I think that psychotherapists need to be analysed. My answer is that most people who take up psychotherapy as a major part of their professional lives do feel the need to explore their personal problems in this way at some time during their careers. Moreover, doctors are better doctors if, at some time, they have had to be patients; and I think it is valuable for psychotherapists to be exposed to psychotherapy in order to make it easier for them imaginatively to enter into what their patients are experiencing. Psychotherapy is difficult to teach, and personal exposure as a subject is a good way to learn something about its practice. However, there is no study known to me which shows that psychotherapists who have had psychotherapy are more effective than psychotherapists who have not. There are some people who seem to be natural psychotherapists; who are gifted with intuition, empathy, and compassion combined with the necessary degree of detachment; and I am far from suggesting that highly skilled, sophisticated psychotherapy can only be practised by those who have been through a full-scale analytical training.

I turn now to the effects of practising psychotherapy upon the psychotherapist. First, I would like to emphasise that it is an intensely interesting and rewarding profession. What other occupation can permit one to get to know, extremely intimately, so large and so varied a collection of people? Second, it is obvious that it is a pleasure to feel that one is valued by, and some help to, one's patients. However, I am not primarily concerned with extolling the merits of the profession, but with looking at effects which are not always clearly seen.

Since the practice of psychotherapy demands some of the traits of personality that I have outlined, it is natural that these should be reinforced. There comes a point at which a certain kind of therapist may almost disappear as a definable individual, in rather the way that some self-sacrificing, Christian ladies become nonentities; people who are simply there for others, rather than existing in their own right. When psychotherapy is practised every day and all day, there is a danger of the therapist becoming a non-person; a prostitute parent whose children are not only all illegitimate, but more imaginary than real. Psychotherapists tend to forget that, although they probably get to know their patients better than anyone else, they see them under special conditions for only a short time. They do not see their patients in action in the external world; and, naturally enough, hear more about their anxieties, failures, and hesitancies than they do about their successes. In imagination, therefore, they may have a somewhat distorted picture of them as less competent than in fact they are. However, living vicariously, through one's patients, is as much a danger for some psychotherapists as it is for some parents; and it is essential for the therapist to find some area in which he lives for himself alone, in which self-expression, rather than self-abnegation, is demanded. I agree with Thomas Szasz when he writes: 'If you see eight or ten patients day in and day out, the chances are that the level of your work may not be consistently high. A good solution to this dilemma is to combine analytic work with other activities compatible with it, for example, with teaching, research, or writing.'[14]

I also want to draw attention to the fact that the families of psychotherapists tend to suffer; for two reasons. First, professional discretion means that the therapist is virtually unable to discuss his work with his family, who often have very little idea of what his work entails. If either parent is a full-time, or even part-time therapist, this means that interchange with the family is diminished, to the disadvantage of both sides. If the most important thing which has happened to one during the day is that a particular patient has shown a sudden improvement, or that another has broken off treatment, being unable to talk about this 'in front of the children' may increase a parent's remoteness and make the children feel excluded. I often wonder whether the families of spies, or even of politicians in possession of State secrets, who constantly have to watch what they are saying, suffer similarly. Of course psychotherapists are likely to discuss some aspects of cases with their spouses, who are also required to be discreet: but I have generally been extremely reluctant to go into any details, feeling this to be a breach of confidentiality, although most patients seem to expect that one will talk about one's work to one's wife, and I always answer truthfully about this if the subject is raised.

The second reason that the practice of psychotherapy may be deleterious to family life is that, since psychotherapy is an emotionally demanding profession, the therapist may well have little emotional energy to spare for wife and family. If, all day long, one has been listening to the troubles of others, one is less likely to be patient with the tribulations of one's spouse, or with the ups and downs of one's children's school lives, than if one was employed by an insurance firm. Some psychotherapists want to escape into something quite impersonal. I found my own interest in reading novels greatly curtailed when I was in full-time practice, although I have learned much from novelists about human nature.

Another danger is what Jung called 'unconscious infection'. However balanced the therapist may be, he is likely to encounter a few patients whose material is both particularly disturbing and fascinating, so that his own equilibrium is threatened. I am not referring to the danger of falling in love with the patient, since this is a well-recognised risk which applies not only to psychotherapists but to doctors in ordinary practice, clergymen, and many other counsellors of various kinds. What I have in mind is something to do with unconscious areas within the therapist's own psyche which, in ordinary life, might never have been stirred up, or even seen the light of day in his own personal analysis. I decided many years ago that I was not going to be one of those bold analysts who undertake therapy with psychotic patients; for although I believe that the majority of such patients are not suitable for psychotherapy of an uncovering kind, I do recognise that a few are, although their treatment is generally difficult and time-consuming. I simply found that close encounters with schizophrenics seemed perilously upsetting. Bertrand Russell said of his friend the novelist, Joseph Conrad: 'He thought of civilized and morally tolerable human life as a dangerous walk on a thin crust of barely cooled lava which at any moment might break and let the unwary sink into fiery depths.'[15] In intimate contact with psychotics, I felt the same. If a therapist finds himself threatened in this way, he should talk it over with a colleague. He might find that further analysis for himself was called for: on the other hand, he might have to recognise his own limitations.

Another danger for the therapist is that of being cut off from contact with ordinary people. Some analysts are quite unable to communicate with anyone other than patients and other analysts. These are the analysts who spend eight or more hours per day seeing patients and then, when evening comes, dutifully attend an analytic seminar. Such a life diminishes one as a human being, besides reinforcing the esoteric, dogmatic and faith-like aspect of some analytic groups to which I have already drawn attention. I think it very important that therapists have as normal a social life as possible, in which they meet as friends people in entirely different walks of life who pursue entirely different vocations. Some psychotherapists carry their professional set into ordinary life to such an extent that they are unable to distinguish people whom they really like and find interesting from those whom they do not.

However, I do not want to end by leaving an impression that psychotherapy is so full of dangers that I deter anyone who is likely to be good at it from taking it up. Psychotherapy, like other professional activities, has its disadvantages; but its interest far outweighs them. Human beings are endlessly fascinating; complex amalgams of all kinds of qualities, good and bad. There is no trait of personality, no human characteristic, which does not have two sides to it. If I had to choose one overriding impression which I have received from my practice as a psychotherapist, I would point to this ambivalent complexity. My life has been greatly enriched by my profession; and I am grateful for having had the opportunity of penetrating deeply into the lives of so many interesting, and often lovable, people.

References
1.   Hudson, Liam *The Cult of the Fact*, p. 83. London: Cape.
2.   Dent, James K. (1978) *Exploring the Psycho-Social Therapies through the Personalities of Effective Therapists*, p. 73. U.S. Dept. of Health, Education and Welfare. Nat. Inst. of Mental Health, Maryland.
3.   Rogers, Carl (1951) *Client-Centred Therapy*, p. 21. New York: Houghton Mifflin.
4.   Skinner, B. F. (1971) *Beyond Freedom and Dignity*, pp. 200, 205, 177, 164, 160. New York: Knopf.
5.   Berlin, Isaiah (1976) *Vico and Herder*, pp. 23, 28. London: Hogarth Press.
6.   Dennett, D. C. (1973) 'Mechanism and Responsibility' in *Essays on Freedom of Action*, ed. Honderich. London: Routledge.
7.   Rapoport, Anatol (1960) *Fights, Games and Debates*. p. 306. Ann Arbor: University of Michigan Press.
8.   Wolberg, Lewis R. (1978) *The Technique of Psychotherapy*. Part I, pp. 331–2. New York: Grune and Stratton.
9.   Dent, James K. op. cit, p. 94.
10.   Parker, G. V. C. (1967) 'Some concomitants of therapist dominance in the psychotherapy interview.' *J. of Consulting Psychology*, 31: 313–318. Quoted in Reisman, John M. *Toward the Integration of Psychotherapy* (1971) New York: Wiley.

11.   Parry, John (1967) *The Psychology of Human Communication*. London: University of London Press, pp. 170–1.
12.   Rycroft, Charles (1968) *Anxiety and Neurosis*, p. 78. London: Allen Lane, The Penguin Press.
13.   Cohn, Norman (1957) *The Pursuit of the Millennium*. London: Secker and Warburg.
14.   Szasz, Thomas (1965) *The Ethics of Psycho-Analysis*, pp. 219–20. New York: Basic Books.
15.   Russell, Bertrand (1956) *Portraits from Memory*, p. 82. London: Allen and Unwin.

15

Solitude, Interests and Healing

Since this is a book about individual psychotherapy, its emphasis has been upon the therapeutic interaction between the psychotherapist and his patient, rather than upon internal processes of healing taking place within the isolated individual. Preparation of a second edition gives me the opportunity of adding a chapter which draws attention to some of these processes. In Chapter 8, I wrote: 'Transference, (and I am now using the term in its widest sense, that is, as comprising the whole gamut of the changing relationship between the patient and the therapist) is the most important single factor in therapy.' I still believe this to be true; but I have also come to realise the importance of other factors in healing which are not so closely connected with a person's relationships, either with a therapist or with others. Because modern techniques of psychotherapy have concentrated upon object-relationships, we have tended to forget that relations with other people do not constitute the whole of any person's significant experience. Freud defined psychic health in terms of the ability to love and the ability to work. Psychiatrists and psychoanalysts have emphasised the former at the expense of the latter.

For many people, intimate personal attachments certainly are the mainspring of their lives; the most important determinants of happiness or unhappiness. But this is not true of everybody; and, even those who are fortunate enough to have satisfying intimate ties with their families and others, generally spend a good deal of their time in occupations and pursuits which do not involve close relationships. Interests, both those comprised under the heading 'work', and those which people pursue during leisure hours, enrich a person's life. They may even be a main factor in preserving mental health. The assumption that intimate personal relationships constitute the only road to happiness is unjustified. Although analysis of transference may be the most significant factor in healing, there are also other internal factors which operate within the psyche of the isolated individual which tend to be neglected. Because individual psychotherapy is essentially an interaction between persons, we pay less attention to those insights and changes of attitude which come about when people are alone and undistracted. In the practice of psychotherapy, it is important that these internal processes be recognised and promoted, and that time and opportunity be given for them to proceed.

In mental hospitals and other institutions for the emotionally disturbed, therapeutic emphasis today is upon group participation, milieu therapy, ward meetings, and staff-patient interaction. Even occupational therapy and art therapy often take place in a group setting. Every possible means is employed to ensure that patients are kept in constant contact with each other and with the nurses or other staff. This incessant social activity is probably beneficial in the case of schizophrenics who might otherwise withdraw from social interaction. But I doubt if it is the right regime for every kind of patient. Some patients not only desire solitude, but need it. In the nineteenth century, the American neuropsychiatrist Silas Weir Mitchell instituted the 'rest cure', which involved removal from relatives and partial isolation. This technique afforded opportunity for quiet reflection; and allowed a natural scanning and sorting process to take place within the patient's mind which often put into perspective emotional problems which had previously seemed threatening.

Scanning and sorting takes place in the mind during sleep, and may be one reason why sleep is necessary. During the day, most of us are exposed to a sensory input which might prove overwhelming if we could not retreat into the solitude and quiet of sleep. It is well known that depriving subjects of sleep is a rapid method of inducing mental stress and malfunction; and acute outbreaks of mental illness are often heralded by a period of insomnia. We do not fully understand the mental processes which go on during sleep; but they are certainly important for the preservation of mental equilibrium. Many people have had the experience of being unable to decide between two courses of action, and of going to bed with the problem still unresolved. On waking, the solution is often obvious. Conventional wisdom has always recommended 'sleeping on it' when faced with a difficult dilemma, and conventional wisdom is right. This is one commonplace example of problem-solving taking place within the isolated individual, without reference to relationships with others.

Psychotherapists will frequently encounter patients who have been bereaved, and who are finding it difficult to come to terms with loss. As Colin Murray Parkes has indicated in his excellent book *Bereavement*,[1] bereaved people who have received specialised counselling or psychotherapy show better health and adjustment a year after their loss than those who have not received such help. He also comments on those cases in which mourning has been incomplete because, at the time of the loss, the subjects had bottled up their feelings, shown very little emotion, and perhaps deliberately kept themselves so busy and so engaged with other people that they had not allowed themselves time and opportunity to experience their grief in its full intensity. Mourning can be a very long process; and although confiding in a psychotherapist can speed the process to some extent, the hour or two per week which the psychotherapist can offer is not enough to encompass all the problems posed by the loss of someone who played an intimate role in every aspect of the bereaved person's life. In dealing with such patients, it is important that the psychotherapist should be aware of the many ways in which patients prolong their grief by never really facing it. He should also encourage such patients to spend at least some part of the day alone, in order that they may be able to allow their deepest feelings to manifest themselves.

In Chapter 6, I referred to a patient who suffered from recurrent psychotic breakdowns, but who gained considerable benefit from writing a book about her illnesses instead of continuing to pretend that they had never happened. Similar considerations apply to the bereaved; and those who, when alone, can bring themselves deliberately to recall the details of their relationship with the deceased, the good and bad times spent together, the ups-and-downs which are part of every intimate relationship, will find that they come to terms with loss more quickly than those who avoid their memories. If bereaved people feel inclined to write an account of the deceased person, so much the better. Many families have unpublished memoirs which, even if not of general interest, are enthralling to their descendants. Some of these memoirs, which are often undertaken shortly after death, not only preserve the memory of the deceased, but must have provided a therapeutic resource for the bereaved.

In Chapter 6, I made passing reference to encouraging depressed, middle-aged patients to recall the day-dreams of their adolescence, and suggested that it was often fruitful to revive interests which had been allowed to lapse during the busy years of raising a family and establishing a position in the world. For example, a woman who has had to devote herself to the care of children during most of her adult life may find herself depressed when they no longer need her. Perhaps, as a girl, she had some interest in art, in music, in gardening, or in dressmaking which the demands of her family stifled. People often believe that, when they reach middle age, it is too late to pursue interests which absorbed them when young; or feel that they will be unable to learn anything new. Such a conviction may be part of their depression; but it is also the case that people generally underestimate the capacity of older people to achieve success in whatever field they choose to employ their talents. Grandma Moses did not have her first solo exhibition until she was 80, and went on painting until she was 100. Many similar examples will be found in Jeremy Baker's book, *Tolstoy's Bicycle*,[2] which is so named because Tolstoy did not have his first bicycle lesson until he was 67. Most psychotherapists, because of their concentration upon object-relations, underestimate the importance of interests in the economy of the psyche.

One exception to this generality is Morris N. Eagle, a Professor of Psychology at York University in Toronto, and author of an excellent book, *Recent Developments in Psychoanalysis*.[3] In 1981, he published a paper on *Interests as Object Relations*.[4] In this paper, he disputes the conventional psychoanalytic notion that interests are the product of diverting sexual aims to 'higher' pursuits; that is, that they are the result of sublimation. He points out that research has demonstrated that even very young infants discriminate between various auditory and visual stimuli, and show preferences for particular colours and shapes, as if they were orientated toward an interest in non-personal objects from the beginning of life. Moreover, both infant monkeys and infant humans show attachment to objects which provide comforting contact, irrespective of whether such objects also relieve hunger and thirst. Eagle concludes: 'All the evidence taken together indicates that an interest in objects, as well as the development of affectional bonds, is not simply a derivative or outgrowth of libidinal energies and aims, or a consequence of gratification of other needs, but is a critical independent aspect of development which expresses an inborn propensity to establish cognitive and affective links to objects in the world.'[5]

People who know nothing of psychoanalysis will think this conclusion banal. Ordinary observation demonstrates that the majority of people have interests of some kind, ranging from stamp-collecting to music; from fishing to playing the stock market. Common sense disputes the idea that such interests are derivative; diversions of sexual energy away from its basic aim. But Freud was so persuasive, and so certain that he was right, that he convinced generations of psychotherapists that sexuality was the basic motive force within the psyche, and that anything which mattered emotionally must be sexual in origin. Freud actually wrote: 'Originally we knew only sexual objects;'[6] a conclusion which objective studies of the behaviour of infants does not support.

Since psychotherapists are predominantly concerned with

interpersonal relations, it is all the more important for them to realise that, as Eagle points out, abiding interests and values can also provide 'something to live for'. Indeed, Bettelheim and others have shown that, under the appalling conditions prevailing in concentration camps and prisoner-of-war camps, those who survived were those who were devoted to ideals and beliefs which transcended the life of the individual. We know that, when one partner in a long-term relationship dies, the survivor is more likely to become ill or to die than others belonging to a similar age group. But those who are fortunate enough or provident enough to have developed some passionate enthusiasm unconnected with their partner will have something to live for which will see them through their mourning.

The creatively gifted often use their work rather than their interpersonal relationships as their primary source of self-esteem and personal fulfilment; a subject which I have explored at greater length in my book *Solitude*.[7] Eagle quotes the case of a composer whom he knew for many years who was 'frequently paranoid, oversuspicious, chronically over-vigilant, showed extreme mood swings, had periods of intense anxiety, and reported quasi-hallucinatory experiences'.[8]

Yet this very disturbed individual never broke down. Eagle was convinced that his musical gift and passion played a central sustaining role in his life, and that, without it, he might well have become psychotic.

It is not difficult to believe that interests, like music, literature, and painting may be the hub around which the life of a creatively gifted person revolves. But those who are not particularly gifted are also orientated toward the impersonal as well toward the personal. The English passion for gardening sustains and enriches the lives of many people who have no intellectual pretensions; and the same is true of fishing and other pursuits which enliven the weekends of those who are working, or alleviate the tedium which may afflict those who have retired.

As we have noted, the majority of psychotherapists have been far more concerned with object-relations than with the internal processes of integration which take place when the individual is alone. One notable exception to this generalisation is C. G. Jung. Jung died in 1961. Virtually the whole of his later work is concerned with what he called 'the process of individuation'; that is, with the individual's quest for wholeness and integration conceived as an internal process, with little emphasis upon his relationships. Jung, like other analysts, formulated his ideas on the basis of his clinical experience. It is no accident that Jung specialised in the treatment of older patients. The people who most interested him were mostly middle-aged and over; whereas Freud thought that patients near or above the age of fifty were unsuitable for psychoanalysis. It remains true that Freudian psychology is predominantly concerned with childhood and youth, whereas Jungian psychology is chiefly orientated toward later life. Jung's patients were often people who had married, raised a family, and attained a certain position in the world. Then, perhaps after going through a mid-life crisis, as Jung himself had done, they sought therapy because their lives seemed meaningless and empty.

Jung maintained that the problems of the second half of life were of a different order from those of the first half. A young person's psychological task is to emancipate him or herself from Oedipal ties; to find sexual fulfilment, found a new family, and gain a position in the world. But, supposing a person has achieved all this and yet, when reaching the threshold of middle age, finds nothing but dust and ashes?

Jung found that, by encouraging such patients to record their dreams and phantasies, a process of internal development was set in motion which, in favourable cases, culminated in a new attitude to life characterised by acceptance and equanimity. Jung advised such patients to set aside a part of the day in which they could be quietly alone, and then to enter a state of reverie, in which consciousness is preserved, but in which judgement is suspended. The patient was enjoined to note what phantasies occurred to him, and then to let these phantasies pursue their own path without conscious interference. Jung called this process 'active imagination'.

It is worth remarking that Jung's attitude to phantasy is the opposite of Freud's. Freud linked together play, phantasy, and the dream as escapist manoeuvres designed to avoid reality. He considered that these three activities were an expression of 'primary process'; that is, of mental functioning governed by wish-fulfilment and the pleasure principle. Freud thought that these essentially childish or primitive mental activities should be outgrown and replaced by 'secondary process'; that is, by rational thought governed by conscious planning and the reality principle. Jung, on the other hand, encouraged his patients to make use of 'primary process', because he perceived that phantasy could be creative rather than merely escapist. Jung found that, by getting in touch with the irrational, imaginative aspects of his psyche, the patient not only rediscovered elements of his personality which had been neglected, but also came to realise that his own ego could never be paramount, but was always dependent upon integrating factors which could not be consciously contrived.

It is worth noting that the state of reverie which Jung encouraged his patients to enter is exactly the state of mind in which most creative discoveries occur. Although there are few instances of new ideas stemming directly from dreams, the majority of creative people describe solutions to problems or new inspirations occurring when they are in a relaxed state of mind in which they are not deliberately directing their thoughts, but passively allowing thoughts to occur to them. Jung discouraged his patients from thinking that the phantasy material which they produced was in any way related to art, because he wanted them to retain spontaneity by not attempting to order or shape the material. Nevertheless, active imagination and the creative process are closely similar, and Jung recognised this when he wrote: 'My aim is to bring about a psychic state in which my patient begins to experiment with his own nature – a state of fluidity, change, and growth where nothing is eternally fixed and hopelessly petrified.'[9]

The psychiatrist in training, for whom this book is primarily written, may not find that he encounters many patients of the rather esoteric kind described by Jung. Most of the people whom he will be asked to treat will be suffering from neurotic symptoms which are more specific and more easily definable than a general sense of emptiness and futility. But Jung's way of treating this specialised clientele is important because it directs our attention to the fact that healing processes go on outside the psychotherapist's consulting room. Patients can be encouraged to speed the processes of self-discovery and self-healing by employing the technique which Jung describes. In urban life, it is often quite difficult for people to find any part of the day during which they can be alone or find time for reflection. It is important that they do so. Even if a man or woman works all day in a busy office, and then comes home to a house full of children, it is usually possible to arrange to go for a solitary walk, or to insist upon being undisturbed for a limited period. The current interest in, and enthusiasm for, the various techniques of meditation bear witness to the therapeutic value of periods of solitude in which the business of life is temporarily brought to a standstill.

Western cultures tend to overload the sensorium. In cities, it is impossible to avoid the noise of motor traffic, railways, and aircraft. The telephone is a threat to privacy. We are so accustomed to constant auditory stimulation that many seem to be uncomfortable without it. Although driving a car is an opportunity to be alone which some people prize as an opportunity for reflection, others feel so bereft that they are uncomfortable unless listening to the radio or cassette player, or talking on the car telephone. In recent years, various techniques using diminished sensory input have been found to be therapeutically useful.

The appropriate acronym REST stands for Restricted Environmental Stimulation Therapy or Technique; a term which has replaced the often misused designation 'sensory deprivation'. Two procedures are in current use. The first consists of secluded bed rest in a completely dark, sound-proofed room. The second adds to darkness and silence flotation in a warm saline solution, which further diminishes sensory input by reducing proprioceptive information from the trunk and limbs. There seems little doubt that these techniques induce profound relaxation and feelings of well-being in the majority of volunteers who have experienced them. In the early experiments with sensory deprivation, some subjects reported visual hallucinations, whilst others experienced acute anxiety or attacks of panic. More recent research indicates that these negative effects are rare, and that many of them may have been due to inadequate preparation of the subjects. The persons most likely to react unfavourably are those suffering from claustrophobia, and obsessive-compulsive neurotics.

In Chapter 13, I suggested that psychotherapists were best at treating the inhibited and overcontrolled type of person, and less successful at helping those who suffered from eating disorders, or who smoked and drank excessively. It is therefore of signal interest that REST has been particularly successful in treating this latter group of problems; 24 hours of REST, whether or not combined with an anti-smoking message, resulted in an average 38% reduction in smoking which persisted three months later. Reduction in alcohol intake amongst heavy drinkers has also been reported; as has weight loss in the obese, and weight gain in the anorexic.[10] There is also some evidence that REST increases the flow of new ideas.

Although more research is needed, the evidence strongly suggests that REST ought to be available in psychiatric hospitals and clinics as an adjunct to psychotherapy and as a therapeutic resource in its own right for addictions and eating disorders. In this chapter, I have referred to sleep, to withdrawal into solitude, and to reverie as being states which promote internal processes leading to problem-solving, to the development of new attitudes, and to healing. It is of great interest that REST techniques appear to speed these processes, and also that the same circumstances favour creative discovery.

Because the process of psychotherapy is often a compelling journey of exploration, both patients and their therapists are inclined to believe that what goes on during the hours of therapy is overridingly important, and that anything which takes place outside those hours is of less significance. This belief is sometimes justified; but it may lead to undervaluing any efforts at self-exploration and self-understanding which the patient may undertake when alone and not involved directly with the therapist. Jung always required his patients to do 'homework'; and, in our present circumstances, in which psychotherapy is a scarce resource, so that we cannot give each patient as many hours per week as we would like to do, it is particularly important that psychotherapists should realise how much can be accomplished by patients working at their problems on their own. There is a sense in which psychotherapy is never completed; but it often sets in motion a process of development which, one hopes, may continue throughout the subject's life. Jung thought of neurosis as a person finding themselves 'stuck'; that is, as having reached an impasse in life in which change and development was halted. As the quotation given above indicates, Jung's goal in psychotherapy was not to reach some chimerical goal of complete cure, but to bring about a state of fluidity, change, and growth. If psychotherapy enables the individual who was 'stuck' to travel hopefully, the psychotherapist can rest content. The only final solution to the problems of living is death. While life itself lasts, we must accept that we never achieve complete integration or perfect adaptation. There is always another step to be taken, or a new problem demanding solution.

References

1. Parkes, Colin M. (1986) *Bereavement*, Harmondsworth: Penguin.
2. Baker, Jeremy (1982) *Tolstoy's Bicycle*, New York: St. Martin's Press.
3. Eagle, Morris N. (1984) *Recent Developments in Psychoanalysis*, New York: McGraw Hill.
4. Eagle, Morris N. (1981) *Interests as Object Relations*, Psychoanalysis and Contemporary Thought, 4, pp. 527–565.
5. Ibid., pp. 537–538.
6. Freud, Sigmund (1912) *The Dynamics of Transference*, Standard Edition, Collected Works, Vol. 12, p. 105, London: Hogarth Press and Institute of Psycho-Analysis (1958).
7. Storr, Anthony (1988) *Solitude*, New York: Free Press also published in (1989) *Solitude*, London: Collins.
8. Eagle, Morris N. op. cit., p. 532, n. 2.
9. Jung, C. G. (1931) *The Aims of Psychotherapy*, Collected

Works, Vol. 16, p. 46. London: Routledge & Kegan Paul (1954).

10.   Suedfeld, Peter (1982) *Aloneness as Healing Experience*, in *Loneliness*. L. A. Peplau and D. Perlman (eds.). Chichester: Wiley.

Further Reading

Casement, Patrick (1985). *On Learning from the Patient.* London: Routledge.

Casement, Patrick (in preparation). *Further Learning from the Patient.* London: Routledge.

Flach, Frederic (ed.) (1989). *Psychotherapy*, Directions in Psychiatry Monograph Series, No. 5. New York: W. W. Norton.

Hobson, Robert F. (1985). *Forms of Feeling: The Heart of Psychotherapy.* London: Routledge.

Holmes, Jeremy and Lindley, Richard (1989). *The Values of Psychotherapy.* Oxford: Oxford University Press.

Malan, David H. (1979). *Individual Psychotherapy and the Science of Psychodynamics.* London: Butterworths.

Storr Anthony (1973). *Jung*, Modern Masters. London: Fontana.

Storr Anthony (introduced by) (1983). *Jung: Selected Writings*, Fontana Pocket Readers. London: Fontana.

Storr Anthony (1989). *Freud*, Past Masters. Oxford: Oxford University Press.

Index